SALVATORE

REVENGE IS A MUST

CHARLES CAMPO

DENVER, COLORADO

Salvatore

REVENGE IS A MUST

SALVATORE LEANED HIS exhausted body against the tunnel wall, dropped his pick and wiped the sweat off his brow. He closed his left eye and peered out of the corner of his right eye, as he attempted to observe Michael, but the beads of sweat streaming down his forehead immediately made contact with his open eye. Wincing, he wiped his brow again and calmly waited for Michael's comments.

"Sleeping again?" questioned Michael with an especially loud emphasis on the latter part of his question. "Damn the day that my sister married a cucumber like you.'"

"Damn the day that I, Salvatore Campo, married a Moccia. You are all slightly touched in the head."

For several long moments, the two friends stared at each other in utter silence; then, suddenly, they burst into wild fits of laughter. Unable to control himself, Michael fell to the ground holding his stomach.

"You should have seen your face," laughed Michael.

"My face?"

Salvatore and Michael were the type of childhood friends who had constantly competed against each other; yet, this rivalry, if one may call it that, had never wrecked their relationship; in fact, it had generated a fondness rarely seen in these parts.

Considering the time and place, the rarity of their relationship was questionable. They were Sicilians; as such they had faced the onslaught of nature, poverty, and war as a cultural habit; somehow it was easier to face such tribulations in two or three. Families and friend were a serious matter, and as friends go, Salvatore and Michael were an exemplary pair.

Strength through unity was hardly a figure of speech, but a way of life amidst the troubled islanders. Camaraderie was a crucial element of their lives, one that eased the pains of existence a bit. Unity was a necessity born out of misery.

In other times or in other places, perhaps, these men may have been entrepreneurs or landowners. Sicily, however, offered them only physical labor for enough compensation to keep them alive-barely. Yet life must go on, and, having no choice, the men did what they had to do in order to feed their families.

Salvatore straightened his tall, lean body while running his calloused hands through his thick black hair.

"Today must be the hottest day of the summer," said Salvatore while wiping the sweat from his moustache with the back of his right hand.

"Yeah, yeah, get to work, you bum!" teased Michael.

Returning himself to his pick, Salvatore gazed at Michael in such a manner that Michael's attention was immediately drawn to the possibility of Salvatore's retaliation. While Michael nervously watched Salvatore in an attempt to anticipate the various possible tricks Salvatore would play on him, Salvatore picked away at the sulfur.

Today, he had worked six hours. Six more killing hours until quitting time. The heat, the fatigue, and the stench made working conditions sub-human, but one had to eat and his family was not small. Calogero was six, Tina ten, and Lucio thirteen, and the two youngest, Pino and Rosetta next year, Lucio would be fourteen and could come to the mines with him. Thank God for that, thought Salvatore. Thank God!

Then, there was Grazia. Never complaining, always trying to make the best of every situation, she was the driving spirit of the family. What would he have ever done without her?

When he had married her he had wanted her to have so many things, but poverty, like a terrible storm, wiped clear the mere thought of such dreams. Campo had often wondered whether she had ever resented her situation, but her face would never reveal any such emotion. Her great beauty, mysteriously, sustained itself through her tough years. She loved Salvatore (much to her parents' despair) and would have no other man.

Not that Salvatore wasn't handsome, but he was church-mouse poor. Often the thought of depriving Grazia had entered his mind in the first years of their marriage, but with the arrival of the children, Tina's illness, and his long, brutal working hours hardly allowed him to concern himself over these doubts. Yes, most of all, it was the work at the Trabonella mines that drained most of Salvatore's energy. There was no leisure to question, debate or dream. One only accepted and told oneself the little lie: Things could be worse.

Working with friends such as Michael and Franco minimized the drudgery, but the heat, the damn heat was unbearable. It was a light-less heat that penetrated every pore; a heat that exhausted one physically before one even began any sort of activity. Breathing became difficult, as well as eating or drinking. Every activity was hampered by the constant, ever-present heat.

Other than his friends, Salvatore would start chipping away at the sulfur, he would establish a pattern between his breathing and the chipping that would totally absorb his attention. Placing his left foot in front of his right foot, he would take a short breath as he raised the pick above his head. Then, at the top of his stroke, he would inhale, again, preparing for the attack. Finally, while forcing the air out of his lungs, he would blast the rock with his pick. Inhale, inhale, exhale. Up, hold, down. Inhale, inhale, exhale. One, one, two.

The lantern overhead cast a shadow against the wall as he went through the motions, but being unable to watch the shadow move in its circular path; Salvatore would imagine the creation of a perfectly timed, circular pattern. As time progressed, the machine would become the wheel of a train-not a train to take him to distant lands, but just the wheel, moving in place, over and over and over again. Inhale, inhale, exhale. The day would whisk by him as he kept perfect timing. Often he could pass several undisturbed hours in this manner.

"What the hell is wrong with you?" Michael would say, after trying to get his attention.

"Nothing, just thinking," would be Salvatore's usual response.

"You're always just thinking!"

Salvatore would nod, and then attempt to get back to his rhythm. Up, hold, smash. Inhale, inhale, exhale. That was his rhythm. It worked well.

Today, however, he found it difficult to concentrate on his wheel. The air was so dry that it scorched his lungs as he inhaled; it broke his concentration. Picking at the sulfur seemed to get him nowhere; the rock was like steel, unbreakable. The fatigue, the heat, the pain in his arms and shoulders served as a nasty reminder of each passing second. Time seemed to be crawling.

The heat of the tunnels was far different than the heat of the outside world. Lacking light, smelling of stale, overused air, the tunnel was like a dark inferno - a sensation that remained with Salvatore for hours after leaving work.

When he had been a carrettiere near Enna, he hadn't really minded the heat because of the light breeze that would intermittently cool him. In addition, the sights were so beautiful, the days so care-free, that it seemed like a dreamy paradise compared to the hell of the mines.

Modern technology had replaced the need for the carrettiere and now, he was reduced to smashing rocks in the dark, and, without Baptista.

Baptista had been Salvatore's horse, his friend, and, his bread and butter, for he wouldn't have been much of a carrettiere without a horse. In fact, it had been Baptista who had first started Salvatore on the rhythm.

While travelling the endless kilometers among various villages, he would watch the wheels of the wagon spin. Curiously, he had noticed, these wheels seemed to stay in place. Simultaneously, the sound of the horse's hooves slapping the ground allowed Salvatore to daydream endlessly. Clip, clip, clop.

In the early part of the summer of his seventeenth year, he had bought Baptista, and for very little money, because she was thought to be a sickly animal. A little care, however, proved fruitful; she turned out to be a strong healthy horse.

This marriage of faithful beast to loyal man had been fabricated in heaven. They had a splendid relationship from the very outset. As long as he would groom her daily and give her the usual over-feeding of sugar cubes, she was content. And that meant that she worked. At first, Salvatore tried to be the strict master, but Baptista proved to be much more stubborn than he, and, as a result, she won every single war, battle or even skirmish. But the affection was by no means one-sided. Salvatore's friends, Michael and Franco, often noticed the reverence which the horse's expression could take on in the vicinity of her master. His wish, along with a sugar cube, was her command.

These years when he was hauling sulfur and grain around the Villarosa area, he and Baptista were as talked about as were the soccer games. This wasn't true just because they were bringing goods, but mainly because of the special air that would surround the pair as they clip, clip, clopped into the village. Clip, clip, clop--she had given him the rhythm. Clip, clip, clop - inhale, inhale, exhale.

"Damn this heat!" gasped Salvatore.

Michael stopped working and leaned on his pick, the sweat pouring down his long black hair, past his forehead, and eventually on the ground. He growled, "Where is Franco with our food? I need a rest and I'm starving. Where is he?"

"Here I am," said a voice behind Michael.

As Michael turned around, Salvatore quickly kicked the bottom of the pick which was supporting Michael. A look of anger swept across Michael's face as he hit the sandy ground, but this expression quickly changed into laughter as he realized that Salvatore had been avenged.

"Okay, peace," laughed Michael.

"Peace? This is only the beginning," teased Salvatore.

Attempting to get up, Michael squatter as if ready to lift his torso straight up, when a hand from behind him grabbed his shoulder and pulled him backwards. Sprawling backwards, he looked up to see Franco's laughing face.

"I give up. Today is not my day."

"Oh, yes it is. Wait until you see what I have brought you for lunch," said Franco. "We have bread, mozzarella, and my best wine."

"Now you're talking," Salvatore said as the two of them began sitting down against the tunnel wall preparing for lunch.

"I'll have you know that my wife stayed up late last night preparing these lunches," stated Franco proudly.

"Well, she must have stayed up real late. Sandwiches are so hard to make," teased Michael.

"C'mon, stop it. Angelina is proud of that bread. Her bread is not like the bread found in these parts.

"Who is bringing lunch tomorrow?" questioned Franco.

"He is!" snapped Michael, teasingly.

"What do you mean, it's your-"

"I know, I know," said Michael as he bit into the sandwich.

The three famished men devoured their food in silence. Salvatore cherished these moments with his friends, these boisterous, sometimes silent but pregnant moments of communication, of unity. Gazing upon Franco, he thought of the many experiences the three of them had lived through. The trio had been inseparable for over two decades. Franco's cool-headedness had helped them escape from some rough situations, as had Salvatore's intelligence and Michael's strength. They complemented each other perfectly, three sides of the perfect triangle.

Alone, trouble might find and overcome them, but together they were able to surmount any obstacle, for any characteristic one lacked for a given situation, one of the other two was bound to have. "The trinity," was what the people used to call them. Salvatore smiled -- the Father, Son, and Holy Ghost.

"Well, who will get here first to occupy our land, Patton or the Americans or the English?" questioned Franco.

"Who cares? Nothing will change anyway. We will still serve the conquerors."

"You are crazy, Michael," retorted Salvatore. "The Americans are going to be for us. They have lots and lots of money which they easily throw away. You should hear what my cousin says about New York. There are big streets, big houses, and big beautiful cars - all this in New York. There is incredible wealth everywhere."

"All that is important is that they don't close the mines," stated Michael rather blandly. "The mine is our incredible wealth."

"No way. Why should they do such a thing? The owners will still need sulfur to be mined. The world doesn't end because of a change in power. Who should know that better than we Sicilians? Anyway," continued Franco, "we shall see what happens."

"The owner is friendly with the Germans. He will have to leave if the Americans come," responded Michael.

"That doesn't mean that the Americans won't take over the mines. They aren't rich because they waste good resources. This mine is a valuable resource. Everyone needs sulfur."

"Yeah, I suppose: so, but-"

"Hey!" screamed a voice from somewhere down the tunnel. "What is this, a party or something? Get to work."

Furious, Michael jumped up and yelled, "We are eating lunch if you don't mind."

"Don't take all day, then. It's a lunch, not a grand banquet that you have in there."

"Cangeliera, that bastard," responded Salvatore

nonchalantly as he continued with his lunch.

"His job!" screamed Michael. He felt Franco's hand on his shoulder indicating for him to drop the matter.

After several long minutes of silence, Salvatore, with a mouth full of food, looked towards Michael.

"Patton will get her first. He's smarter.

"Yes, maybe, but when will he get here? The Americans have been coming for the last thousand years," said Michael.

"Thousand years," chucked Franco.

"Well, who knows what's going on? Maybe the Germans are putting up a hell of a fight. They can't win, though, because the Americans have much more money. Money wins wars, not good generals and soldiers."

"Sure, Salvatore, you and your cousin," teased Michael.

"My cousin? What does he have to do...?"

"What are you doing?" screamed Cangeliera at the trio.

Standing not more than four feet from the group, the supervising laborer, Cangeliera, fumed over them like a monster.

"You have been bullshitting around for at least an hour. What are you, the three new owners?"

"An hour!" yelled Michael. "We just sat down!"

"Yeah, sure. Look, we aren't paid to play games. Franco, get into the other tunnel," ordered Cangeliera, adding with a chuckle, "You boys must be separated."

Salvatore stared Michael down with such intensity that Michael relaxed before his temper had a real chance to flare. Franco picked up the papers that his wife had wrapped the lunches with and proceeded apologetically towards the other tunnel.

The other tunnel was dreaded, even by the most skilled miners. There was hardly any light in the labyrinth. It was far from being safe. The walls deep in the tunnel grumbled from time to time. Above all, however, there was the solitude. Franco was the only man to work the other tunnel, since it was a fairly new tunnel and was only in the exploratory stage. Cangeliera had all the remaining laborers work in areas where the sulfur was known to exist. Cangeliera used the mine assignment as his ultimate power-play to show who commanded.

Salvatore had always thought Cangeliera jealous of the trio's camaraderie. It was possible that the superior was just doing his job, but his picking on Franco was unpleasant. Franco never complained - as Michael or Salvatore would have.

Slowly, Salvatore and Michael rose, cleaned up their papers, dusted the dirt off their pants, lifted their picks, and began mining again.

Michael stared in the direction of Cangeliera as the supervisor walked triumphantly away. After several moments, he started laughing.

"He knows I'll bite his elephant ear from his cucumber head if he dares to say anything to me. Why doesn't he leave Franco alone? What a bastard!"

"Cangeliera is not such a bad guy," said Salvatore. "He probably figures that we won't work hard if we are together. He's just doing his job as best he can."

"Well, then why doesn't he ask me to go into that damn tunnel?" Michael asked, pointing in the new tunnel's direction.

"Because he...."

"Yeah, yeah, sure," said Michael, obviously annoyed.

The men continued to work in silence for some time. Salvatore was thinking about his dinner at home, his wife, and his children. Lucio would be a problem. Next year he would be able to work in the mines, but he wants to remain in the schoolhouse studying. Real brains come from living, thought Salvatore, and not from reading dumb, fantasy-filled books. Books were the devil's invention.

Salvatore had always tried to be a good father to his children. Lucio should be able to study, but the family desperately needed the extra income. Tina was not a healthy child -- the medical expenses were becoming outrageous. Certainly, Lucio could work for a few years and then go back to studying, thought Salvatore.

"I don't know what to do about Lucio."

"What did you say?"

"I said that I don't know what to do about Lucio."

"Lucio? Oh that. Drag his ass in here next year. That's all you do."

"It's not that easy. Don't you understand that I want him to have a better life than mine, that-"

"Bullshit'." interrupted Michael. "He's Sicilian and poor. He will always be that way. No matter what you do, you can't change destiny. Don't let your foolish cousin convince you of those American dreams. He's probably starving in New York."

"Oh come on! You can't be that pessimistic on everything. You have to hope...without hope we are worse off than the poor jack asses."

"Look Salvatore, the only thing you hope for is that you don't die while your family is still young. As long as I'm strong, I can feed them. Hope, you say? I hope, yes I hope that I can feed my family for as long as possible."

"But don't you want your sons not to have to see life in that way? Don't you see that all we are doing by having children is passing on misery? We must do something to permit them to have some choice, some decision-"

"Choice? They have a choice; work or starve. That's-"

"Look, don't interrupt me," said Salvatore, visibly angry. "I think that we must do something to spare our sons this life worse than hell itself."

"Can I say something?" questioned Michael.

"Yes, go ahead."

"Thank you. What will you do if Tina's condition gets worse, huh? Don't you see that we are all trapped in what we are - poor and Sicilian? We have no escape route."

"You are truly crazy. Why are you so bitter about everything?"

"Why, you ask. Well I'll tell you. Nobody is ever going to put it up my ass, Salvatore. You know what I mean? Nobody!"

"I just can't believe-"

"Don't then," screamed Michael. With his face flushed, his temper about to burst out of control, he took a deep breath and then resumed his labor.

Salvatore, assuming the conversation had ended, let out a long sigh and then looked over at Michael.

"I'm sorry, I didn't mean to-"

A giant shake and loud crashing noise startled Salvatore. He looked at Michael, and the panic-stricken look on his friend's face shocked him.

"Franco!" screamed Michael as he threw his pick down and raced for the mouth of the semi-virgin tunnel Franco worked. Salvatore stood frozen momentarily, then began running after Michael. His heart pounding loudly, Salvatore felt a myriad of confused thoughts whip across his brain. Panic-stricken, he rounded the last corner before the entrance of the new tunnel to see some fifteen men gathered there. Dust was pouring out of the tunnel. Salvatore finally noticed Michael beating people out of his way in a futile attempt to enter the tunnel. It took four men to hold Michael back. Cangeliera and two others had already entered the tunnel in order to rescue Franco; it was deemed foolhardy for anyone else to take chances with his life. When the earth growls, it too must eat - -and it devours the enemy who sticks iron into its vitals.

Years flew by Salvatore's mind; he broke out in a cold sweat. Michael paced the tunnel entrance, swearing, crying, pushing men aside. He was being spoken to be Santo Bellaria, Cangeliera's best friend. Ballaria's attempt to calm Michael was futile, though it did help to relax Salvatore.

The tunnel had probably caved in at the far side,

thought Salvatore. More than likely, Franco wasn't even scratched, and they would all laugh this incident off in the evening. We will have some good laughs and wine, thought Salvatore, and joke about the nine lives all miners have - like Nero, company cat, who escaped all perils. Franco is all right. Of course he is.

"Hey Michael. Come here for a minute," entreated Salvatore.

Nervously looking about him, Michael walked quickly towards Salvatore. Looking into Michael's uncertain eyes, Salvatore said, "Franco is alright, calm down."

"He's dead, I'm sure of it!" screamed Michael hysterically.

"What a ridiculous thing to say."

Michael had run back to the tunnel entrance hoping to hear, see, or sense some news about his friend. Suddenly someone inside the tunnel yelled that they had found Franco. Cangeliero and his men were coming out. Salvatore let out a huge sigh of relief as the men began to cheer loudly.

"I am sure Franco is all right," said a man behind Salvatore.

As Salvatore was patting Ballaria on the back, he noticed that Michael's expression hadn't changed. Walking towards his friend, Salvatore smiled at Michael's reactions. Such an incredible temper, always thinking the worst, constantly worrying - that was Michael. Even as a child, Michael always had been pessimistic and his temper - he had such a temper, had gotten many little boys beat up.

"Come on, Michael. He's all right," said Salvatore as he put his arm around Michael's shoulders. Michael was stretching his neck into the tunnel in order to be the first one to see Franco. Just like a kid, thought Salvatore, smiling. He suddenly felt Michael's shoulders lunge from under his arms. Michael picked up Cangeliera as he was walking out of the tunnel and slammed his head against the wall. Cangeliera bent over to cover his stomach only to feel Michael's powerful fist smash into his face.

Salvatore, shocked, totally confused, stood completely still as he watched three men attempt to restrain the madman, but Michael's incredible strength, combined with threats to the lives of those who touched him, permitted him to strike Cangeliera several times too many. Screaming like a maniac, Michael was finally wrestled to the ground, but carefully so, for every man who aided in this process seriously feared Michael's vendetta.

Outraged, Salvatore walked towards Michael. What in the hell was wrong with him? Not even when someone had disputed the sanctity of his sister (a deadly thing to do in Sicily) had he been so cruel and just plain crazy.

Salvatore thought that maybe the heat and the tension had been too much for Michael. This was the final straw. He would surely be fired for this incredible behavior. Cangeliera wouldn't forgive and forget his battered face. No way!

"What the hell is wrong with you?" screamed Salvatore at the crying Michael. Perplexed, seriously worried over his friend's condition, Salvatore bent over to hold his friend, but Michael began pounding the ground while screaming like a demon.

"Help me Santo," ordered Salvatore to Bellaria. "Help me calm him down. I've never seen him this way. Let's get him outside. Come on, help me!"

Reluctantly, Bellaria slowly walked over towards Michael.

"Grab his legs and I'll…"

Suddenly, he saw Franco and understood all. Clutching his throat in a futile attempt to restrain his own vomit, Salvatore fell to his knees. The last image in his brain prior to his fainting was Michael's pounding on the ground.

Lying some twenty feet from Michael was a very battered, very dead Franco di Stefano, his eyes still fully open.

CHAPTER **TWO**

"SALVATORE, SALVATORE," ECHOED a voice. "Salvatore, wake up." Startled, Salvatore embraced consciousness as if shocked by an electrical current. The wet rage on his forehead fell to the ground as he attempted to sit up. Feeling immediate dizziness, he slowly returned to his former position.

"You have been out for almost an hour," whispered Santo Bellaria.

Smelling the sickening order of vomit, Salvatore's perplexed mind tried to piece together those tragic events he had just experienced. As one recollects a nightmare, Salvatore found himself unable to understand the consequences of the accident; his entire being assumed a disbelieving, numb state. Ever so slowly, though, the vivid reminder of the incident, the smell, would force his brain to concentrate on what had happened and what it all meant.

He would have to be the one to tell Angelina and the children. What would they do without a man in the house? Salvatore shuddered as his train of thoughts began to accelerate. The consequences were unthinkable but predictable; it was one of those rare, unexpected situations that completely destroyed people's worlds. What would his family do?

The intense grief over his good friend's death was unbearable: It was well beyond tears. A person around whom one plans the future, whom one sees as naturally always being there, creates an unbelievable void upon his sudden exit. The suddenness was the real burden. When his father had died, he had expected it for years. Such preparation, although not being an end in itself, lessens the pain of the momentary loss of an indispensable loved-one.

"Your father has just died," said Dr. Angiello upon leaving the other room of Via Provenzano Number 18. At the time, some three years before, Salvatore couldn't imagine any greater pain possible; but now this, this lightening void, this total collapse of his universe was too much pressure on him.

Such a young man, such a vital spirit, such an undeserving candidate to die. Why? Why him? What had he ever done wrong? What would his family do? What would he and Michael do? One; can pose the questions easily enough, but there are no believable answers, no satisfying solutions.

Salvatore attempted for the second time to sit up. Wavering for a few moments, he, with the help of Bellaria, managed to stand up. Stumbling over towards the water buckets, he picked one up and poured the water on his head, hoping that the pain and the stench of vomit would simultaneously disappear. The stench did.

He turned his aching head in the direction of the tunnel of doom, and saw Michael kneeling beside Franco's body. It appeared to him that Michael was whispering to

Franco. Although he could not hear what he was saying, he could see Michael's lips move and his facial expressions go through an animated series of contortions.

Thinking back on his reaction towards Michael's behavior, Salvatore felt deeply ashamed. Restraining himself from crying, he walked over to Michael and placed his hand on his shoulder.

Looking up at Salvatore, Michael's worn eyes had an empty, bland look that frightened Salvatore.

"I'm going to Franco's house," said Salvatore.

"I can't, I just can't, I-"

"It's all right. Why don't you go home, Michael? You could use some rest. We all can."

Michael nodded as he turned his head towards Franco. Suddenly jumping to his feet, Michael glanced at Salvatore, then back to Franco, and then ran out of the tunnel.

Salvatore watched his friend run out of the tunnel. Michael would suffer the most. Shaking his head as if expecting to wake up from a nightmare, he noticed the battered Cangeliera sitting on an upside-down water bucket.

"No need to say anything. I understand totally." whispered Cangeliera so that the others couldn't hear him.

"You are a good man, Antonio Cangeliera, a good man."

Nodding, and then putting his hands in the bucket of water, he splashed his face.

"You see," moving his jaw around with his right hand, "it's not broken. Strong-jawed family, we Cangelieras are," laughed the supervisor.

Salvatore patted his supervisor on the back, and then turned towards Bellaria.

"I must go speak to his family."

"I don't envy you. This is all so horrible. He was such a good man, an honest man, a hard-working man. Oh, what a day, a horrible, horrible day. We know the dangers we face in this rat hole, but still can't accept them when Nature cashes in her chips on us."

Of course he was an honest man, thought Salvatore. Isn't it bizarre how all men are good, honest, beautiful people when they are dead? Such a good man. They hardly knew him. Hello, goodbye, was their relationship with his good, honest man. Death makes saints of us all.

Checking his rising anger, Salvatore exhaled slowly. Looking at Franco for the last time, he could still perceive the outline of the handsome smiling boy. Lying there, lifeless, battered, he seemed unperturbed by his death. Calm, cool-headed Franco. Even in death, he was still the same man.

Salvatore exploded into a mass of hysterical tears. All the emotions of the afternoon seemed to converge on his eyes as he cried furiously, unashamed, for several minutes. No one approached him, and the communal empathy for him was manifested by the workers' immediate withdrawal. The last time Salvatore saw Franco was a sacred moment that he would keep close to his heart for the rest of his life.

It was nearly dusk when he approached the last hill. From his present position, he could see the collapsed section of flue on Franco's roof struggling to remain intact. Franco had been born in that house, thought Salvatore. As boys, Franco, Salvatore, and Michael had often played in that garden. They had even built a tree house that was destroyed by a storm the day after they had completed their masterpiece. Franco wanted it high to see the river. For weeks, the boys had been cutting wood. After much planning and four or five false starts, they finally built it -and then the storm totally destroyed it. They had felt so badly that Franco's father gave them an extra amount of fruit.

Every day, Franco's father would bring the boys a bowl of fruit, the best fruit in Sicily. Salvatore thought he could still taste the delicious red oranges, the wonderful golden grapes. Oh those grapes I They would eat them in such quantities that they would become ill. Every time the trio had those incredible stomach pains, Michael would swear that he would never eat any more golden grapes. Everyone agreed. The next opportunity, however, they forgot their vow.

Salvatore laughed out loud as he thought about their grape ritual. How sick they used to get!

So many experiences had they gone through together that it was impossible for Salvatore to recall an experience that didn't happen with all of the trinity present. Except of course, the Baptista incident.

Baptista, oh my God, what about Baptista? A broad smile spread across Salvatore's face as he recalled the first time he had entered Franco's gate with Baptista. He had been so proud, such a big man he was: He owned a horse. Franco's awed expression had quickly changed to one of nonchalance, for he hardly wanted to appear impressed.

"So you got a horse, huh?"

"Yep. A damn good one, too."

"How much?"

"Two hundred lire," lied Salvatore, afraid that the actual low price would suggest to Franco that he had bought a ton of future dog food.

"Two hundred?" retorted Franco, unable to disguise his amazement.

"Yep."

At that point, Salvatore's cockiness had reached such a point that it would take a major eruption from Etna to bring him back to earth.

"What do you know about horses, anyway?" asked Franco suspiciously.

"Everything. This horse will pull any load for me. She is a strong, beautiful animal," answered Salvatore while patting his horse on the mane.

"She is that strong, huh?" teased Franco.

"Any load that a.-horse can pull, Baptista can pull. She will do it for me," reported Salvatore proudly.

"Well, she can surely plow a field, then."

"Of course," said Salvatore with increasing uncertainty, as he began to understand the trap that Franco was quietly setting for him.

"Good. My father wants me to plow the back lot. Baptista can do it in no time; then we can go to the village and see the girls. What do you think, Salvatore?"

"Well...."

"Great. Hitch her up to the plow and we'll get started right away. Come on, hurry up."

Slowly, Salvatore began hitching up Baptista. Giving her several sugar cubes, he begged her to live up his boasting or, at the very least, not to make a total fool out of him. Baptista, however, held different ideas.

As soon as Franco began to plow the field, she became very excited. At first she was amused by the novelty of the task, but soon, very soon in fact, she became thoroughly bored, even annoyed by the whole matter, as though she were meant for grand parades and military ceremonies.

Suddenly, she galloped down the hill. Fortunately, Franco's harness slipped over his head as she made her surprised escape. Racing across the field, she started towards the vegetable gardens. Horrified, the boys watched Baptista pull the plow through the vegetable garden, destroying everything in her path. Fences, vegetables, fruit trees, herbs, and the venerable old scare-crow were torn as Baptista circled to make yet another path of destruction. She was evidently having a grand old time. Franco and Salvatore were not.

By the time she was reentering the garden, the entire di Stefano family was out of the house screaming like madmen. Either being very brave or very stupid, Baptista continued on her rampage as if nobody was there.

Salvatore screamed, or attempted to, as Franco's father picked up his ancient shotgun. Baptista, showing that her motivation was not stupidity, immediately raced down the hill towards full protection and safety.

"Jesus Christ, I thought she was a work horse. What is wrong with that monster?" yelled Franco.

Several months of free labor finally enable Salvatore to pay off the full damages caused by Baptista. Included in this punitive deal was a harsh whipping of the two boys by their respective fathers.

Much of the remainder of the day was spent by Salvatore in an attempt to recover his frolicking steed. Finally, when she had become hungry and tired, she came back to Salvatore acting as if nothing had happened.

Salvatore's smile quickly disappeared as he entered the gate of the di Stefano's residence. Not knowing what he would say or do once he met Angelina; he forced himself to continue walking towards the house. His heart beating loudly, he felt like death approaching his next victim. Shaking noticeably, he walked through the open doorway: two soft oil lamps momentarily caused him to lose focus on the room.

Angelina was seated in a rocking chair mending a torn shirt, probably Franco's. Her long, brown hair extended part her shoulders out into the air. She was slightly bent over, concentrating deeply on the task at hand.

The stove was active as smoke travelled up through the chimney. The sound of boiling water indicated that pasta would soon be ready.

Franco's children were seated on the ground whispering childhood fantasies to each other.

Except for the stove, the chair, and a crude table, the main room of the house was fairly barren. Two small windows on either side of the doorway were the only additional source of light.

He walked several steps into the room; his concentration was interrupted by loud laughter coming from the children. Angelina looked towards the children smiling then noticed Salvatore.

Now shaking uncontrollably, Salvatore attempted to speak, but his throat was so dry that he could manage only a cough. Sweat poured down his face and he extended his trembling hand towards Angelina, and then quickly pulled it back to his side. He burst into tears, unashamedly and vigorously.

Angelina quickly understood the1 situation. Her deep brown eyes had recognized the grief in Salvatore's expression. Her husband must be dead. Like a large chandelier crashing in an otherwise still room, her world collapsed about her.

Tears began to stream down her face as she stared into Salvatore's troubled eyes. After several moments, she wiped her tears discreetly and told her children to go outside to play, to spare them the initial shock.

Salvatore attempted to speak, but Angelina motioned for silence. Looking slowly around her, she appeared to be imagining the house without Franco.

"Was it painful?"

"No."

"We will have a proper funeral in two days."

"Angelina, I want you to know that I will do anything in my power to help you and-"

"I know you will, Salvatore."

She motioned for silence as she began crying. For hours, they sat together, not speaking to each other but simply crying, expressing their great loss, their enormous grief. She retained a firm grip on Franco's tattered shirt, half-mended.

"Why? Why him?"

Salvatore stared into her eyes, wishing he could somehow take her pain away.

"How did it happen?"

"The mines, the new tunnel caved in. It happened so quickly,"

For the next several hours they discussed the tragic events of the day; the children returned, were told, but were too young to fully comprehend. They would understand soon enough, though.

Salvatore left when Angelina fell asleep. Upon his return home, he was greeted by his wife, who had been mourning Franco's death. Bad news spread rapidly.

His wife left the house to attend to Angelina. Softly asking his children to go outside, Salvatore sat down at the table and looked around his room. His exhaustion and the void he felt in his gut made his environment appear hostile; the moonlight poured into his worn eyes as the volume of the night sounds seemed outrageously high.

He grabbed a wine flask, and poured a glass full of blood red wine, and gulped it down. Deciding that the only way he could sleep was to be totally drunk, he poured many glasses of wine into himself. Finally, in a drunken stupor, he fell asleep, only to be confronted with horrible nightmares.

The morning of the funeral was unbearably hot. Arid, scorching air bleached all that was visible.

Proceeding behind the wagon containing the coffin, the friends, relatives, and neighbors of Franco di Stefano paid their last respects. Wearing the traditional garments of mourning, the people followed the wagon as the black witness of death slowly wandered towards the cemetery.

Franco di Stefano, the good, honest Franco di Stefano, was buried on August 29, 1904.

CHAPTER **THREE**

"SALVATORE! SALVATORE, HURRY up! We'll be late for work."

"Wait a minute, I'm coming, I'm coming," replied Salvatore as he hurriedly threw his coat over his shoulders, kissed his wife goodbye, and ran out into the cold, early morning weather.

Michael, impatient as ever, was waiting some twenty yards down the road. Approaching him, Salvatore noticed an excitement in Michael's expression that far surpassed his usual nervous state.

"Wei], what's with you this morning?" asked Salvatore.

"The Americans are coming. They have invaded. The Germans are leaving. Can you believe it?"

"Wait a minute. Hold on. Now slow down and tell me what's going on," said Salvatore with ever-rising excitement.

"Let's start walking, though, we're late. My cousin, Giuseppe, told me this morning. He said he saw some German troops moving rapidly to the north. They are leaving the island!"

"So Patton will get here first after all! What did I tell you? I should have been a military man."

"Yeah, sure. You know, maybe the war will be over soon-"

"It won't make any difference. We are always in one war or another," interrupted Salvatore, realizing that he sounded like Michael.

The excitement over the invasion had generated the first sign of life in Salvatore in weeks. His inability to cope with the void left by Franco's death had taken its toll. He had lost ten pounds and hadn't slept soundly in weeks. Constantly drinking, he had become the worry of everyone from his immediate family to his fellow workers. Michael had even argued vehemently with him on several occasions, pointing out that Franco wouldn't have wished for such a reaction.

Of course, Michael was right, thought Salvatore, but it was so difficult to live with the pain, that awful pain. Somehow, the wine made things easier. At night he would toss and turn for hours at a time. Finally, he would arise and drink himself to sleep. His health had begun to suffer from this condition as had his family life. It wasn't fair to his family, and he knew it.

The Campo and Moccia families had decided to aid Franco's family in every possible way. This meant less food for everybody, but the Campo's and Moccia's were more than happy to aid their friends in distress. Even Lucio, hoping to please his father, had decided that he would begin work in the mines the following year, but Salvatore would do anything for the family of his deceased friend. Thank God for the mines!

Michael and Salvatore continued discussing all the various possibilities and implications of the American invasion as they finally approached the work site. As they rounded the last bend before the main road that entered the site, they were startled by a loud commotion. Breaking into a run, they were greeted by a group of miners standing about sixty feet from contingent of Gendarmes.

Cangeliera, standing on the worker's side, was screaming insults in the direction of the Major, obviously the man in charge.

"You are a pack of heartless thieves! How are these men to survive? Tell me Major, you have a fine education, you are a man of the world, what are we to do? Maybe we will eat at your house, Major," yelled Cangeliera in an embittered tone.

Despair quickly enveloped Salvatore. These last few weeks had been a continuous nightmare; he was hoping someone would awaken him gently and reassure him that it had all been just a bad dream. But there they were the Gendarmes. They were closing the mines I Why? What was the damn reason?

"What the hell is going on?" screamed Salvatore hysterically at Bellaria and Cangeliera.

"These sons of bitches are closing the mines I Can you believe it? The owner is leaving and has decided that we all can die, for all he cares. Can you believe it?"

The major, sitting on his horse, began laughing at this point.

"I'm going to kill him," whispered Michael to Salvatore as he pulled out his knife and started in the direction of the officer. Salvatore pulled Michael back.

"Stop it, you fool. They'll kill you first. What will your family do then, when you are dead, huh? You idiot! They are just doing their job."

"Oh, the hell with their job!"

Michael, realizing his folly, put the knife away, but then he gave Salvatore a hard look.

"They don't have to do it, do they? They don't"

"Listen, Michael. We will figure out something to do. Don't worry, I'm not going to let my family and Franco's family starve. Just don't do anything stupid. Leave it to me."

Michael's anger was dissipated like a balloon that lets out air when pricked. Salvatore's good reasoning made perfect sense. How glad he was that his friend was so calm in the face of disaster.

"Wait here, Michael."

Salvatore slowly walked through the agitated mass of workers and headed in the direction of Cangeliera. He didn't really like dealing with him, but many of the men listened to Cangeliera, and, in essence, he was a good man. Maybe.

"Cangeliera, Cangeliera, come here please for a moment," motioned Salvatore. "I need to speak with you."

Cangeliera walked quickly over to Salvatore.

"Listen," whispered Salvatore drawing Cangeliera closer. "Take the most trustworthy men you can find and meet me at dusk at Michael's house. I have a plan, but we mustn't talk about it now. Is it agreed?"

"What sort of plan are you talking about?"

"Don't worry; we'll talk about it then. Please be there," said Salvatore. Turning his back on the perplexed Cangeliera, he slowly walked back towards Michael.

"What did you ask him?"

"Ask him? I told him to bring some good men to your house at dusk. I told him I have a plan.

"What plan?" questioned Michael puzzled.

"I don't know right now but I'm sure I'll think of one by dusk."

"That's great! Fantastic!" snapped Michael. "You tell him you have a plan and-"

"Calm down. I'll come up with something good; you'll see. Let's get out of here before real trouble starts."

The two men quickly turned around and walked back in the direction from which they had come. The sun was getting stronger and the early morning mist had all but disappeared.

Salvatore began to feel better; with various thoughts racing through his brain, he had little time to ponder the tragedies that had confronted him. He knew he couldn't let his family and friends go hungry. And frankly, he felt a twinge of pride in the manner in which he had dealt with Cangeliera. We must act, and act soon. But what would he tell them at the meeting? What should they do? Possibly he could ask the Mafioso, Lipani, for advice, but he lived too far away to be worthwhile at tonight's meeting. Well, he would just have to think of something.

"I think we should bring my brother to the meeting, said Salvatore. He is bound to lose his job at the granary."

"Yes," said Michael, "Let's go talk to him now. We could also get Giuseppe Spilatieri to come."

"Of course. He may have an idea, since you don't," teased Michael.

"We shall see. We'll see tonight."

After ten minutes, they arrived at the granary. Deciding that it would be most prudent to let Salvatore go in alone, Michael sat down under a tree. Salvatore entered the granary and asked to speak to his brother; his excuse was that it concerned urgent family business. Approximately twenty minutes later, Salvatore returned with a big smile on his face.

"I told him to bring Spilatieri. He was so curious, you wouldn't believe it."

"I can just imagine. Listen Michael, I'm going to go home. I'll meet you at your house around six o'clock. All right?"

"All right. See you then."

As he watched Michael disappear around the bend, Salvatore wondered what his family's reaction would be. Angelina and Franco's children, he hoped, wouldn't take it too hard. He had silently promised Franco at his funeral that he would always look after them, so they really didn't have to worry. Of course, they would be frantic.

Walking slowly up the hill towards his home, Salvatore began to think of a plan of action. Removing his cloak due to the increasing heat, he decided that somehow, some way these people were going to eat. All the workers were honest men, but if the landowners were going to force their hand, the men would have to resort to stealing. Steal from the rich! The noblemen of Sicily would have to feed us; we have fed them for a long time and now it's their turn to feed us, thought Campo. We cannot starve. Our families will not starve. They are innocent. They have suffered.

Many such thoughts entered Salvatore's mind; he quickly became depressed. If the men would have to resort to being criminals in order to survive, what would that mean for their families? Obviously, the men would have to be constantly on the run. He would dearly miss his wife, his children, and his home, but such sacrifice was necessary for the good of the ones he loved.

As he prepared to walk into his home, he realized that his outward appearance on this situation must conceal his true feelings if he were to lessen not only his family's anxieties, but ultimately that of his comrades. Somehow, Salvatore felt like a general leading his men into a suicidal battle.

"Salvatore, what are you doing here?" asked the startled Grazia Campo. "You've been fired?"

"No," he said softly. "They have closed the mines. We are all out of work."

"Oh my God!" gasped Grazia, "What are we to do now? What can we do, without the mines we're done for?"

"Now, now, stay calm. We are going to find a solution to this matter. In fact, I'm going to look for a job this evening with the farmer Tramontano. I know I can find some tiling fast. Everybody knows what a good worker I am," replied Salvatore.

"Everything will be all right. I promise. Don't worry and don't tell the children. The children don't need to see our fears."

Sitting at the table with Grazia's eyes upon him, he

reiterated his assurances as Lucio walked into the room.

"What are you still doing here?" he asked.

"They've closed the mines for a day in honor of the American invasion," stated Salvatore. After a few tense and silent moments, Salvatore stood up and walked over towards the stove.

"I'll work on the stove; see if I can get it to work better."

Smiling, Grazia put her arms around him.

"You don't know what to do with yourself, do you? Why don't you go outside and relax while I make a big breakfast?"

"Well, now that you have forced me out of the house," teased Salvatore.

"Go, go out!" laughed Grazia.

By the time Salvatore arrived at Michael's home, it was well after six o'clock. Most of the men were there: Antonio Cangeliera, Santa Bellaria, Michael Moccia, Giuseppe Spilatieri, Carlo Bellaria, Angelo Caruso, Calogero Cimino, Saro Vangone, Orazio Capizzotto, Giovanni Vitale and several others.

The group was fairly agitated, but it quickly stilled itself when Salvatore arrived. He was impressed. Smiling at Michael's obvious anxiety, Salvatore motioned him to his side.

"I still haven't thought of a plan," he teased, truthfully.

"You're crazy, plain crazy!"

"Don't worry," he laughed.

"Don't worry, he says," muttered Michael.

"I think we should start this meeting," stated Bellaria.

"Giuseppe Moccia and I feel certain that we will be fired, so we are behind you all the way," said Spilatieri.

That was it. Why hadn't he thought of it before? A smiling Salvatore had gotten the idea for the plan. The granary! Of course, the granary!

Winking at Michael, he raised his hands and began speaking to the men.

"Gentlemen, we find ourselves in a bad condition. The owner of the mines has let us go to the devil and we have no food or possibility of food for our families. I say that his treatment of us is unfair and inhuman. I say that we deal with his inhumanity and our hunger at the same time."

"What's the point of this?" snapped Cangeliera.

Michael's face lit up like a bonfire. The pride he felt spread all across his happy face. All the men cheered at the idea. They had all come to the conclusion that they would have to steal in order to survive. This was wartime Sicily; unemployment was rampant.

After a brief while of cheering and general discussion, Salvatore said, "Men, we will have to be on the run, for the Gendarmes will chase us. We must spend out last night with our families and meet here tomorrow evening. Make arrangements for seeing them again in a month, but not around here. We should head for the Mafioso, Lipani, to see if he can offer us advice and protection."

"What? Aren't my children flesh and blood? Don't you think; my heart aches when I see the hunting dogs of Cavaliere Mascaro devour rich red meat while my own children know only pasta and some salami? It's not God's will that the dogs eat better than my children. We must accept things as they are because we lack the will to fix things right. My family gets every illness doctored now because we breathe the smoke of wet wood, refusing to leave the stove in our caves we call houses. Yes, caves. I will not honor them by calling them houses. Michael, you don't know how all these things registered in my mind. You have enough anger for the two of us. Lading my hatred for our life upon yours would produce two desperate men. I fear where the desperation will lead us. One of us must command the way or both of us will perish.

The men had naturally realized their plight. The implications were all too obvious; however, the direct manner in which Salvatore had approached the matter had quieted them.

"Let's go to the granary," yelled Cangeliera.

"Remember, at dusk we will meet here," warned Salvatore, and then adding, "Don't forget your weapons."

The next evening the men assembled into something like a single file as they began the descent from Michael's hill towards the granary. Silently, they proceeded toward their goal. Silently, except for Michael.

"I'm so glad the Americans finally invaded," said Michael sarcastically. "We wait for months for the big event, and look what happens. We starve!"

"Yeah, it's kind of funny, isn't it?" mused Salvatore.

Clearing his throat, Michael looked over at Salvatore with a serious expression on his face.

"How long will we have to run?"

Looking into Michael's eyes, Salvatore knew he wouldn't be able to lie to his friend. Recently, times had been so dreadfully hard for all of them, but through all these disasters, they had need for each other: Salvatore needed Michael's strength and urgency while Michael was in desperate need of Salvatore's calm and wisdom. Not that Michael wasn't intelligent; on the contrary, he was an extremely quick thinker; yet, his temper and general state generated some rash decisions on his part. Michael's history had been spotted with various incidents that a cooler temper would have totally avoided. Most of these incidents revolved around Grazia, his sister.

With the exception of Salvatore, Grazia's courting days were non-existent. Though an exceptional beauty, Grazia had a brother whose great strength and violent temper kept everyone away. Actually it was no real surprise that she fell in love with Salvatore, since he was the only man other than her brothers and father whom she saw. Naturally Michael was very pleased to see his sister fall in love with his best friend; however, their parents were, at first, adamantly against any relationship between Salvatore and Grazia. Somehow a marriage between Michael's cohort and Mr. Moccia's prize daughter had not been easy to swallow, but time and patience led the parents to believe that he indeed would make her and them happy.

Grazia's great love for her brother had naturally attracted her to Salvatore. In fact, if it hadn't been for this great love of hers, Michael may have been the most despised brother in history. The fear of Michael's wrath was so strong that Grazia had almost become a dreaded sight, strolling through Villarosa with her girlfriends. This was especially true after the Di Meglio incident, an incident that gave all those who hoped to court the beautiful Signorina a long hard jolt.

Giovanni Di Meglio was one of those bizarre individuals w b had the misfortune of being born a century too late. Short, chubby and balding, the thirty-two year old merchant from Palermo happened, one fine September day, to be travelling through Villarosa on his way to Enna when he spotted Grazia. Standing in the middle of a group of four girls, Grazia appeared to him a vision from heaven.

Rushing to buy some roses, he approached her with the best tender loving look he could form on his face - an expression that was more ridiculous than it was sexy or tender. His first words to her were his revelation of his love for her, to which Grazia replied by bursting out laughing. Being in a totally ridiculous position, but being ever more crazed with his angelic vision, Giovanni Di Meglio stood his ground.

Weeks went by as Grazia was showered with gifts and visits from the well-to-do Di Meglio. Enthusiastic about his financial position, Grazia's parents embraced the merchant; although they were forced to admit that he was a trifle less than desirable. Michael thought him slimy but innocuous, as did Salvatore. Above all, he was considered to be maudlin and a pusillanimous balloon.

Every visit to the Moccia's home consisted of several

fine gifts for the Signorina, a reiteration of Di Meglio's love, a reiteration of her unromantic views of him, and, finally, a tearful departure on the part of the merchant.

"Why do you keep seeing him?" Michael would ask his sister.

"He amuses me, and, besides, he makes me feel important."

"But, you don't love him, do you?"

"Of course not!" she would laugh.

If anything can go wrong it will, and so it was with Giovanni Di Meglio. One hot afternoon he presented Grazia with a rather expensive gift; a carriage with two beautiful white horses. Thoroughly delighted, she immediately wanted to ride in her new toy and so; the two of them proceeded towards the village.

They had a horrible fight on their way to Villarosa. He, totally desperate by this time, pledged his eternal love to her; she snubbed him again. Vowing to commit suicide, he continued harassing Grazia throughout their ride. As they arrived in the village, he asked her to at least kiss him once. Her refusal infuriated him so that he grabbed her and forcefully attempted to kiss his angel.

Shocked, furious, and crying, Grazia jumped off the already stationary carriage and ran frantically away. Realizing what he had done, Di Meglio chased after her begging her to forgive his rash act. As she darted into a small street, the crying, hysterical Grazia ran right into Michael.

By the time she had a chance to realize what was about to happen, Giovanni Di Meglio was running for his life. Michael, tearing away from Grazia's futile grasp, chased after the merchant with a passion rarely seen in runners. Being no match for Michael, Di Meglio suddenly felt two powerful hands violently push him. Literally flying for several feet, the frightened Di Meglio landed on his shoulder and began screaming even before Michael's fist began contact with his body.

It took nearly the entire village; it seemed, to pull Michael off of the bleeding, screaming Di Meglio.

Still half crazed, Michael ran into a woodshed and, to everyone's amazement, came out with an axe and, screaming maniacally, approached the carriage. Hacking the new carriage, Michael screamed insults at the poor merchant from Palermo.

"You're so crazy," laughed Salvatore as the granary came into view.

"What makes you say that?" responded Michael in a mock insulted tone.

"Nothing, nothing."

Shaking his head, Michael came to a halt as Cangeliera called the men over to him for a final talk.

"We will grab the guard from behind and blindfold him. Remember, don't call anyone by name. Take what you can carry and get out of here. Understood?"

"Michael and I will get the guard." said Salvatore.

"Fine. All right men, let's go," ordered Cangeliera.

Silently, Salvatore and Michael crept up behind the guard, pulled a sack over his head, and yanked him to the ground. Tying him up securely and insuring that the guard could breathe easily, Michael and Salvatore joined the other men who had already entered via the main gate. The men headed for the warehouse, where each man took a sack of grain and departed. Salvatore took two sacks, as he had promised one to Franco's family.

"I'll leave the bag with my family. My wife will bring it to Angelina. See you in the morning," said Salvatore.

Hoisting two sacks over his right shoulder, Salvatore walked out of the warehouse. Beginning the long ascent home, he figured he would be with his family in one hour. It would be nine o'clock by then, he thought. Six hours he would have with his family, six more hours with his wife before the chase would start.

Lucio would be the man of the house. Though only thirteen, he was astute enough to understand what was wise for the family; also, he could be used to relay messages between the men and their families, thought Salvatore. He would also take good care of Tina, whose illness required special attention. Somehow, Salvatore had to figure out how to establish logical and safe means of communicating with Lucio.

Salvatore sighed as he put the sacks on the ground and rested for a few minutes. He was on the last stretch before his hill, the hill he wouldn't see for a long time.

How long would this go on? Would they really be able to stop running after the war? Maybe the Americans would declare amnesty for all the men. After all, many families will be thrown into similar positions, thought Salvatore. They can't put us all in jail.

As he entered his home, he put those thoughts aside in an attempt to seriously dedicate these last few hours to his family. Putting the sacks of grain on the table, he embraced his wife. Beckoning her to follow him in silence, he went out in the cool September evening.

"Let them sleep untroubled," he whispered to Grazia.

Clasping his hand, Grazia looked into Salvatore's troubled eyes.

"What have you done?"

"We robbed the granary," he said holding up his hand as a plea to let him explain. "I had to get food to you, for the children, for Angelina and her family."

"But, they'll come after you!"

"I know, that's why I'm leaving in the morning."

"Leaving! Where? Why? What did-?"

"Listen, Grazia, I had to do it. Don't you see, we'll starve otherwise. Everything will be all right in a few months."

"Who told you to do this? Why did you have to become a criminal? WHAT SHAME!!"

Angrily, Salvatore turned to his crying wife.

"Do you think it's easy for me? Do you think I'm going to enjoy being on the run? Being away from you and the children? What the hell is wrong with you? I had to do it and it's done."

The pain in his eyes was inconceivable. Slipping her arms around his chest she cried apologetically. For hours they held each other in silence as if the morning were to bring permanent rather than temporary separation. It would be the first time that they would be separated.

The minutes passed by heavily; Salvatore's anxiety was becoming more unnerving. Fear crept throughout his body as his entire being, dreading the arrival of light, was desperately hanging on to Grazia. She was such a part of him that separation seemed much like physical dismemberment. Their reciprocal dependence had never been really tested; such a test was far from welcome and could have only taken place in a forced situation.

Little Calogero was snoring as Salvatore entered his house. Looking about him as if trying to ensure that none of the details would ever slip his mind, Salvatore felt like crying. He did not. Crying now would have to give way to action.

"When will see you again?"

"On the first of November, send Lucio to former Tramontane. I'll get a message to him and leave money for the family with him. We will meet soon after."

"How do you plan on giving him money? What money?"

"Don't worry-"

"What do you mean? I-"

"I'm sorry," said Salvatore nervously. "I'm just upset by this whole damn mess. Why did this horrible thing have to happen to me?"

"What about Michael?" Grazia asked anxiously.

Salvatore replied by nodding; thereby, indicating Michael's involvement. Naturally, Michael would be involved. Somehow, Grazia had hoped that everyone whom she was close to had not been affected by all the madness.

Ever since Franco's death, the world seemed to be going crazy, thought Grazia. Instead of causing happiness, the American invasion had brought tremendous grief to many Sicilian families. Let's hope they end the war soon. The family would manage, but how lonely it would be?

"I'll think of you every minute," she whispered.

"I love you so much," exclaimed Salvatore embracing the last few moments away with his wife.

Dawn came like a lead weight and with it, Salvatore was gone.

CHAPTER **FOUR**

DAWN CAME ABRUPTLY at Michael Moccia's house. Having spent a sleepless night, Michael welcomed the morning while pacing the floor. Often he would interrupt his pattern to gaze at his wife, then at his children. The sense of sad loneliness he felt had crescendoed with the rising of the sun.

Rosalia, his wife, had finally fallen asleep. The previous night had brought much heartache into the household, but the long hours of crying and the inevitability of the forthcoming events brought about a fatalistic attitude in Rosalia that was, in a way, welcomed by Michael. She was a strong woman, stronger than he in many ways. She had to be.

Many plans had been discussed. They would meet in two weeks at Tramontane's. Michael couldn't wait. Already, he felt as though the separation had been occurring for months. Loneliness, he thought, would be his worst enemy.

Leaving his wife alone in these troubled times was a disturbing thought. Even though the wives would try to look out for each other, the situation was extremely frightening. Most of all he dreaded leaving the children with no father near at hand, remembering how hard it had been for Grazia and him when their father had gone to America. Michael filled his pipe for a smoke; he thought his best with a pipe clenched in his tainted teeth.

For two agonizing years Michael and Grazia had been fatherless. Gone to America to seek wealth, Venanzio Moccia had left his wife and two young children alone. Michael was fourteen at the time, Grazia was eight.

Salvatore was the eternal optimist, always saying that some good would come about out of any situation, thought Michael. Salvatore worried about Lucio working in the mines. What a horrible twist of fate! Not only will Lucio not work in the mines, but neither will Salvatore; Lucio and the rest will only survive by their father's crimes. Michael let out a cold laugh and emptied out his pipe bowl. Such a life, he thought.

Walking over towards Rosalia, he began to sob quietly. Leaning over her, he kissed her lightly on the cheek so as not to wake her. Repeating the gesture with his children, he refilled his pipe bowl. He stood quietly in the middle of the room for a few moments. Closing his eyes, he sighed: then he turned around and walked straight out of the house, gently closing the door.

"Damn!" he exclaimed, emptying his pipe bowl. Looking up he saw the simultaneous appearance of Salvatore and Bellaria. Salvatore approached him slowly. Salvatore's blank expression hardly acknowledged Michael's existence as he dismounted his horse and dropped his body next to Michael. The two men sat in silence waiting for Bellaria's arrival.

The minute that Bellaria had seated himself next to

them, all the other men began to appear at the top of Michael's hill. Slowly, they also began to approach the common meeting ground.

For several long minutes, the men stood about nervously in complete silence. Then, as if aggravated by the silence, Bellaria cleared his throat.

"Salvatore has suggested that on our way to the Mafioso Lipiani's counsel, we should stop at Tramontane's. He may be able to offer us some food and some advice. I think it's a good idea. "What do you think, said Bellaria."

No one answered. The gloomy looks on their faces were unchanged. Cangeliera looked around the group.

"Look, we are all in the same predicament so let's get these stupid expressions off our faces. We have work to do," said Cangeliera rather harshly.

"I think it is indeed a good idea what Salvatore has suggested," continued Cangeliera. "We will need more food soon and we certainly need guns."

"Guns!" interjected Carmine Bellaria, Santo's younger brother.

"Yes guns. This is not a game we're playing. We must be able to protect ourselves and we must be able to force the landowners to feed us. If this is too much for you, Carmine, maybe you should go home and play." laughed Cangeliera.

Blushing, Carmine Bellaria mumbled incoherently and then looked to Salvatore for help.

"Well, I think we are wasting time here. The Gendarmes are bound to find out soon that the granary has been raided, and it won't take them long to figure out who was involved. We should begin to head for Tramontane's farm. Is everyone in agreement?" questioned Salvatore.

Nodding their approval, the men mounted their horses and moved towards the east. It would take them several hours to reach their destination, if they didn't stop too often to rest. Reminding all that the Gendarmes would soon be on their heels, Cangeliera managed to quicken the pace of the group.

Salvatore and Michael naturally, rode side by side. Throughout much of the morning, they had ridden in silence, but the rising temperature made them uncomfortable enough to draw themselves into conversation.

At first they spoke about their families, the anticipated hardships and their feelings of shame. Slowly, unavoidable, the conversation drifted towards the subject of Franco. Actually, it was the first time that they had really openly discussed Franco with each other. As they spoke of Franco, they began to feel better about the situation, not only because they were each other's vehicle for venting their frustration, but also because their own relationship seemed to be getting stronger.

Vowing their eternal friendship to each other, the two friends wondered aloud about the Gendarmes and the horrid situation that faced them, but resolved to continue for the sake of their families.

"I don't want my children to ever have to go through this. Do you see why I wanted Lucio to study instead of working in the mine?"

Michael nodded, and then smiled.

"You know, he will work, though. Such is life for us Sicilians. You know it is so."

Salvatore unwillingly acknowledged Moccia's words. They hardly spoke for the remainder of the day, each absorbed in their own private perplexities.

The sun was high overhead when they approached the farm in Chimera. They had travelled the entire morning without resting. Totally silent, the men decided to rest a spell before they entered Tramontane's home.

Tramontane, the farmer, was a prosperous landowner who hadn't thought of his acquired wealth as due motive for separating himself from his former friends. Throughout the years, therefore, his relationship with Salvatore, Michael, and the others had remained essentially intact. He owned a modest farm that his family had worked for the Delvecchio family for two decades. Sergio Delvecchio, who had recently died, had sold the parcel of rich land at a good price to repay his loyalty to Tramontane. Lacily, the deal had been completed before Sergio's death, because his son, Ettore, was a ruthless bastard.

Of particular note was Tramontane's wife, Maria. A Northerner and the daughter of a well-known pharmacist, she had been well-educated and contained that trait of the truly intelligent person, that of being at ease in anyone's company. Obviously, she was responsible for Tramontane's success, so much so that many spoke of the various accomplishments as being hers rather than his. Her intelligence and wit were legend, yet her humility was much appreciated by the laboring men with whom she came into daily contact.

She was an extraordinarily beautiful woman. Every feature on her face and body was well defined, yet these elements never stood out enough to disrupt the visual harmony that her physique offered. Maria Tramontane was very blond, very Nordic, and extremely rare for Sicily.

Michael thought she was the goddess of beauty, Venus herself. Whenever he was at Tramontane's, he couldn't keep from staring at her and, if not for Salvatore's pinches and kicks, he would have been noticed by her husband. It wasn't that he didn't love and cherish his own wife, Rosalia. But Michael was entranced by such an amalgam of beauty and charm.

Reminding Michael not to visually devour Maria Tramontane, Salvatore led the men past the gates of the farm.

"She knows I want her," laughed Michael.

"She would have to be very stupid not to."

"You know, Salvatore, sometimes I get the feeling that she wants me too. Maybe-"

"Stop it!" laughed Salvatore. "We are going to be guests in his home and you want his wife. Nice guy you are."

Tramontane was sincerely delighted to see his old buddies. Maria, radiant as always, welcomed the men into her home and immediately began preparing a feast for the famished group. The group sat around the root and herb room and discussed their plight. To everyone's surprise, Tramontane was already aware of the incident at the granary.

"The mailman said that a telegram had been sent to the gendarme station in town. They must have notified the Gendarmes in many areas."

"Jesus, they'll be after us soon. What are we going to do?" asked Spilatieri.

"We'll just have to stay ahead of them. That's all," said Salvatore.

"Excuse me," said Maria as she entered the room, "I need some help cutting the chickens. Michael, could you please help me?"

Removing Salvatore's pinching hand from his leg, Michael, with a smile that was impossible to remove, jumped up.

"Of course, it would be my pleasure. I butcher chickens better than Mussolini did the Ethiopians."

"I'll bet," muttered Salvatore as he tried to get Michael to notice his stare. Of course, Michael didn't dare look at Salvatore.

"This kitchen is as big as ray house," chuckled Michael.

"Here are the chickens," said Maria pointing to them, ignoring Michael's opening statement.

Walking nervously towards the lifeless chickens, Michael began to adroitly slice the chickens under the constant visual supervision of Maria.

"Well, how are you, Michael?" asked Maria softly.

"What?" responded Michael too loudly?

Giggling, she reiterated her question.

"Oh then, just fine."

After a long pause he continued.

"Well, not so good. This situation is terrible. You know, I won't be able to see my children, my wife-"

"How is Rosalia?"

"Rosalia? Oh yes, well, she is strong, a good woman. She's taking the situation in stride. I knew she would. Strong woman, she is.

"Yes. What about the children?"

"Fine. Just fine."

Michael continued slicing the chickens as Maria left the room. After several nervous moments, he heard her approaching the kitchen. He immediately looked busy.

"Ah," he said as he noticed her. "Nice chickens you have here."

"Maria, placing her hands on her waist, stared at Michael while smiling broadly. Nervously, Michael observed her stare, and then looked back down at the chickens. Several seconds later, he looked up again to see her staring at him with that irritating, nerve-racking smile on her lips.

He immediately looked away, but feeling foolish, he straightened his body and looked back at her.

"Is something wrong?"

"Wrong?" she questioned. "No, it's just that I wonder why you are so nervous around me."

"Nervous? I'm not nervous-"

"I thought you would like to see what it felt like to have someone constantly staring at you." she interjected teasingly.

"Face it, Michael Moccia." she continued laughing,

"You adore me."

By this time, Michael was crimson. Disbelieving his ears, he had absolutely no idea what to say. There she stood laughing, obviously joking, and he couldn't answer her. Finally, regaining his composure, he said:

"I have a wife and-"

"I'm only joking, Michael," she said. "You are so cute!" she giggled.

Betoldo confesses himself through jokes, thought Michael. She knows that I ... what a fool I am, he thought. Why didn't I think of something to say?

"Where's Franco?" she questioned in an attempt to ease his uneasiness.

"Franco is dead," he answered. "He died a month ago in a mining accident."

"Oh that's horrible!" she said. "What-"

"Please, I'd rather not talk about it," interjected Michael knowing that he had just reversed their roles, as she now felt badly.

"I'm so sorry-"

"Don't worry about it," replied Michael softly. "You are so cute!" he laughed.

"Touché," she retorted admiringly.

Michael smiled and continued to work on the chickens. After several minutes of silence, Michael pointed to the chickens to show that his task was done.

Just as she was thanking him, Salvatore walked in the room. The first thing he noticed was Michael's smiling face.

"He thinks I shouldn't stare at you," said Michael to a

highly embarrassed Maria.

"Michael, please come with me," said the disbelieving Salvatore.

As soon as the two friends were out of earshot, Salvatore grabbed Michael to his side.

"Are you crazy? What are you trying to do? Don't you-"

Holding up his right hand, Michael answered, "It's just a private joke. Just a little fun. Relax Salvatore." He spoke with obvious enjoyment, since the rule was that Salvatore usually told him to relax. Quickly walking away, Michael left the dumb-founded Salvatore frozen in his tracks.

Maria returned quickly to fill another serving board with the rich meal polenta. All her poise and polish proved unequal to seeing Michael again and acting as though nothing existed between them. The simpler Michael played the role more convincingly; only Salvatore saw through the nonchalance of their greetings. In the kitchen as she spread thick tomato sauce atop the meal, she questioned her own feelings about Michael and why she desired him so.

Tramontane was a good provider. Unlike the other landlords in the valley, Tramontane gave his wife full reign of tongue and household management. Tramontane felt inferior to Maria's natural intelligence and grasp of things. Tramontane knows only when to plant and sow, while Maria understood the economics of their farm activities. She admitted that any woman in the province envied her for what control she held. Tramontane placed more and more of the responsibility in running the farm onto her to free himself of the fatigue and strain she took so easily. Maria's control continued beyond the hiring and. farm hands, devising work schedules, and balancing the books; it extended over the full person of her husband, Tramontane.

Tramontane had gotten soft with the riches Maria's shrewd management worn him. Tramontane simply wanted wine, lots of food, and sleep.

Maria could initiate anything, but had no wish to be the leader in her sexual activity with her own husband. To arouse him from his sound sleep would produce nothing. Tramontane's softness involved the inability to become sexually alive. Maria dreaded the litany of excuses he gave for his physical dysfunction. Tramontane cried openly and tried everything his unimaginative mind could suggest to overcome his disgraceful malady. As Tramontane's inability to make love to his wife solidified his largesse to her increased, payment to compensate her for her loss.

Michael's physical power excited Maria to the bone. Sweat beaded on his sinews and clung to the contour of his muscles. Michael's svelte physique revealed itself in his over-washed work clothes. The tightness of his clothing revealed the full measure of the man.

Only once in her life had she known full ecstasy. As a university student her history professor had seduced her in his college office. Maria never thought of reporting the incident to the school authorities because she was honest with herself -- she enjoyed the incident more than she had enjoyed anything in her life. As a virgin and a staunch believer in the idea of purity of mind and body that the nuns had inculcated in her, she had no idea what passion resided in her body. The sensation frightened her because it controlled her. She lived with this secret passion and dove into her studies to sublimate it. Her marriage to the older Tramontane had been arranged by her parents, leaving her no time to give full vent to this strange desire which possessed her. With Tramontane, making love at the beginning of their marriage was a right of man. Then the love-making atrophied into a mild sedative for the insomniac-prone husband.

Maria lived with this wild force. Her imagination and fantasy came to her rescue as she pressed her womanliness firmly into the duck-down mattress against the imaginary Michael or professor who lay in bed with her.

That night with Michael two animal appetites collided into one climactic eruption. Michael took her with a strength and vigor bordering on rape. His kinetic body against hers reawakened every neuron of sensuality she had left in her and revived her dormant passion.

How could she not love Michael? He gave her a gift equal to the jewel tiara Tramontane had created for her in Milan. Michael gave Maria back her gender. All this talk of running the estate linked to her cessation of sexual satisfaction forced her into a masculine domain foreign to her distinct charm and beauty. Michael restored her preferred priority --a woman first, a businessman, second.

"Ah Michael," stated Tramontane as Michael joined his comrades. I'm glad you are here because I have a surprise for all of you. Follow me to the wine cellar."

Tramontane's cellar was of the antique genre; access to the cellar was via a trap door. Once the men stepped down into the dark cellar, they were attacked by all sorts of smells ranging from cheese to wine. It seemed that Tramontane had enough provisions for an army.

Walking to the far corner of the cellar, Tramontane motioned the men over to his side. He opened it. Several hundred German rifles were neatly stacked in the shipping crate.

"How did you get these?" questioned Cangeliera as he picked one up and began examining it, getting oil on his admiring fingers.

"The Germans left rather quickly and-"

"An answer to our prayers!" roared Michael, patting the farmer on the back.

"When we get our hands on some money, we'll relieve you of these rifles," proposed Salvatore.

"Nonsense," said Tramontane. "They are yours. What use does a farmer have of guns? I can't plow with them. Seed I need. Guns are your tools now."

Pointing to several smaller boxes with official German markings, he continued, "There is enough ammunition in there to keep you going in a battle for a year."

The general excitement among the men perplexed Salvatore. Surely they needed the weapons, but they hardly were going to war. He hoped that this acquisition wouldn't lead any of his friends into deeper trouble.

"Open those bottles over on the shelf," commanded Tramontane to Spilatieri. "We must celebrate!"

The men let out a loud cheer as Spilatieri poured wine into their glasses. Laughing, thoroughly enjoying themselves, the group toasted to a free Sicily one time too many. When Maria announced that the food was ready, the men responded with a loud overture to the gracious lady. Smiling, she went back to the kitchen to get more dishes for the table.

Grabbing two dishes full of vegetables; she turned around to see a somewhat drunk Michael. Looking around nervously, he said, "I know I'm a little drunk and that's good because I would never have the nerve to say this otherwise."

"Well, what is it?" she teased.

"I think you are beautiful and I know I love you."

He immediately turned around and started quickly walking back towards the group. Stopping in his tracks when she called his name, he turned around to face her.

"No you don't. You are just drunk." She leaned towards him and kissed him on the cheek. "You are so adorable!" she said bursting out laughing.

Joining her in laughter he sauntered back towards the group realizing how lucky he had been to get out of the mess his rashness had created for him. Wine is man's greatest excuse. Too much wine is man's last-ditch scapegoat.

Sitting about the table, the famished group ate heartily.

"What I think we should do is hit and run," said Cangeliera.

"The only way we will keep ahead of the Gendarmes

is to act quickly and silently like a snake."

"If the Gendarmes aren't already ahead of you," remarked Tramontane. "I would suggest you move south for a few weeks, then reverse your direction and return here. This way I'll be able to monitor their moves."

"How far is Delvecchio's place from here?" questioned Michael.

Tramontane burst out laughing. "Fabulous idea, he isn't even there. Can you imagine his face when he returns to an empty house?"

"Well then we'll do it!" said Cangeliera. "Who will be there, just the servants?"

"Yes, and his wife and children."

"We will take only food and money for our families."

"Everyone agreed?"

"Let's go there now," yelled Michael. "They would never expect us."

"Yes let's go!"

Tramontane escorted his guests to their houses. Thanking him for his hospitality, Salvatore told him that Michael would be by in two weeks, for his wife was to meet him there. Maria was enthusiastic about seeing Rosalia again.

"Thank you for the great dinner," said Michael to Maria.

"You are welcome anytime." As she put her arm around her husband, she winked at him.

"I'm sorry about before," whispered Michael.

Giggling, she waved goodbye to the group and then went inside.

Mounting his horse, Salvatore looked at Michael with questioning eyes.

"What did you apologize for? Was it for what you said to her when I walked into the kitchen?"

"No. You wouldn't believe me if I tell you."

"Try me." said Salvatore.

"Well I told her that she was beautiful and that I loved her."

"You did WHAT?" screamed Salvatore at Michael as he rode off. "Come back here!" Salvatore was laughing wildly.

Michael was way ahead of him trying to imagine Salvatore's reaction. Finally, Salvatore caught up to his friend.

"You know, Michael, I always thought you were crazy, but now I know you are."

"No, not crazy. Just call me Casanova."

"Oh my God!" exclaimed Salvatore.

CHAPTER **FIVE**

IT HAD BEEN several hours since the pack had left the warm, hospitable Tramontane farm. Late afternoon was beginning to offer some relief from the heat of the Sicilian sun. For over half an hour, the men had been travelling through the tall grass, grass that would reach some ten feet high. Half asleep from the large quantities of wine they had consumed, the group travelled in relative silence.

Michael, noticing Salvatore squinting in the direction of the foothills, pulled his horse over and waited for Salvatore to catch up to him.

"What's wrong?"

"Nothing I suppose. There is a strange reflection, as if there were a lake or a mirror over there," said Salvatore pointing in the direction of a hill some five hundred yards from him.

"Where? I don't see anything," said Michael as he began riding again.

"There!" yelled Salvatore. "It's binoculars, that's what it is!"

"Are you sure? Yes … yes … you are right!"

"Michael, keep riding so that they don't realize that we have spotted them. I'll go tell Cangeliera. In about three minutes, Bellaria will pull up next to you. Give him your horse and follow me. Make sure he pulls your horse on the side away from the hills. Understood?"

Michael nodded as Salvatore passed him on his way to speak to Cangeliera. Placing Cangeliera between himself and the hills, Salvatore jumped from his horse. Instructing Bellaria to do the same with Michael, Salvatore waited for his friend to join him.

Deciding to come up the hill from the rear, Michael and Salvatore stealthily sneaked around the hill. In about twenty-five minutes, they could see distinctly two men some thirty yards from them. The two men were lying on their stomachs observing the group through binoculars.

Cocking their rifles, Michael and Salvatore slowly, quietly moved closer to the sentinels. They were able to get so close to them, that they put the hard, cold steel of their rifles on their spines.

"Get up real slowly," barked Michael at the startled men.

Slowly, the trembling boys stood up. Michael began signaling for the others, as Salvatore kept his rifle pointed at the spies. They weren't older than fifteen. Shaking like leaves, they began to cry, begging Salvatore not to shoot them.

"Why were you spying on us?"

"We were told to watch for criminals," answered one of the boys.

"Who told you?" said Michael, harshly. "Who?"

"The Gendarmes, Lieutenant Pavesi ordered us to do it. And besides we lost two of our mules and we thought that the criminals that Pavesi had told us about had robbed them."

"Since when do the Gendarmes tell people what to do?"

Salvatore looked at Michael and laughed.

"What he means is since when do the Gendarmes have civilians working for them?"

"We got caught stealing some..-"

"And they decided to let you go if you helped them," finished Salvatore as Cangeliera and the other men rode up.

"Who are these boys?" barked Cangeliera.

"Spies for the Gendarmes," replied Michael bitterly.

"Shoot them!" ordered Cangeliera.

Michael and Salvatore looked at him as if he were crazy.

"Don't just stand there, shoot them. They are spies."

"You are crazy," said Salvatore.

Furious, Cangeliera reached for his rifle. Before he had a chance to aim his weapon, Michael pulled him off his horse. Holding Cangeliera by the shirt, Michael yelled, 'You aren't going to shoot anybody! Nobody is going to shoot these boys. Do you understand or shall I beat some sense into you?"

Thoroughly humiliated, Cangeliera mounted his horse and silently vowed to avenge himself. Moccia had pushed him too far. The list of affronts grew steadily. While Michael made no conscious accounting to these humiliations he foisted on him, Cangeliera kept careful record. Cangeliera would balance the books someday.

The two crying boys ran to Michael and kissed his hands.

"Get out of here," he growled at them. They ran quickly to resume their boyhood existence.

The men decided to wait a few hours before proceeding towards Delvecchio's estate; they dismounted. Night would be the most opportune time for them to visit the Delvecchio's. They were approximately forty minutes from Delvecchio's home, so they decided to plan a strategic method of attack. They would completely surround the estate and gradually close in. There would be injury done to no one and only enough food and money to sustain themselves and their families would be commandeered.

Salvatore would be the spokesman. Cangeliera, Michael and Spilatieri would ensure that nobody escaped to call for help. The men agreed that the raid must be swift, smooth, and military in its execution.

Salvatore thought it wise to rest a while and think over things after the encounter with the two youthful sentinels. Maybe Cangeliera was right when he wanted to kill the pair. Cangeliera was a realist. We're in this thing for heavy stakes, our lives and the survival of our families; he thought. Salvatore had no schooled philosophy of leadership. What Salvatore did to lead the men was instinctive. Salvatore knew nothing of Machiavelli or that compassion showed confidence and strength. Salvatore was now thrust into a role where what he did had profound effects on many around him, not like his insecure miner's job where his only mental exercise was to decide which vein of sulfur to attack. He liked the feeling of men trusting him and listening intently to his every utterance. No cultural factors prepared Salvatore for his leadership post. The time forced some men to assume the role of leader of men while most cower at the prospect.

The men were tending to the beasts when Salvatore spotted the big wild boar in front of the ancient oak tree. Like most Sicilians, Salvatore loved to hunt. His hunting was mostly as a runner for the landowners who had time, equipment, and the land on which to hunt. As a runner, Salvatore would beat the bushes several hundred yards before the hunting party to spook the game into the path of the oncoming hunters. No question Salvatore had been anxious to squeeze off a few quick rounds on the heavy German rifle. The boar remained still, unearthing wild mushrooms before the oak tree, the tannish board stood out vividly before the deep brown oaken trunk. Without any thought to the shot being heard by police or farmers, he lifted the bulky rifle to his left shoulder, closed his right eye to fix the pig in the chrome sights and squeezed the satiny trigger gently. The pig dropped in his tracks, a direct shot right between the eyes of its massive head.

Bellaria grabbed his donkey's tail to pull its body in front of him as a shield. Bellaria imagined an ambush. Salvatore saw Bellaria1s panic reaction and laughed convulsively. Spilatieri peered from behind a tree and saw Salvatore laughing.

"Go fetch that wild boar I shot for our feast," proudly commanded Salvatore. "No blood-sucking landlord will ever sink his teeth into that juicy meat."

Michael set the party tone by insisting that a pit be built on the spot to roast the prized meat.

Michael raced Salvatore to the fallen boar. "Easy two hundred pounds." assessed the impressed Michael.

The shell had entered neatly between the two glassy eyes, taking with it much of the brain and skull casing.

"With guns like this and a shot like you, we can last forever in those woods," said Michael.

Salvatore tied the pig's front legs together with a strong length of rope and he and Michael dragged the pig back to the makeshift corral where the horses and mules were tethered.

The men eagerly searched for kindling and dead wood to build a fire. Michael placed rocks in a nearby perfect circle to keep the fire safely contained under the pig. Bellaria worked on the construction of a strong spit, stripping saplings of their bark down to their pale green flesh.

Cangeliera gathered the flasks filled to the brim with Tramontane's purple wine. There was ample cheese and bread to accompany the meat. Sebastino left the camp to search for wild figs, berries, asparagus, and nuts which abounded in these parts.

Salvatore also was caught up in the festive spirit. Nevertheless, he took the first watch to keep an eye pealed in the direction of the retreating youth.

Salvatore sensed that the men needed a break in the tension. These were simple peasants used to a structured existence, as predictable as the seasons, as the bills and taxes, and as the suffering and death which was their natural lot. Tense men are unsafe men; they can reunite their souls to the evil everyone has lurking in him. As the band of fledgling aborigines sat awaiting the pig to roast, Michael challenged everyone to an arm wrestling contest. Each member of the band deferred the invitation, knowing full-well the sheer strength of the man. Michael had held the pig full extended in his sinewy arms as Salvatore skewered the beast.

Salvatore called Spilatieri to relieve him of his post.

"Michael, I feel lucky today. Let me have a go at you. I know your weakness," Salvatore spoke out.

"You got to be nuts," retorted Michael. "I'll eat you up alive." Michael gulped down a mouth-full of wine before the bout. Salvatore simply removed his course shirt, hung it conspicuously upon a low branch, and cracked his knuckles noisily.

Michael had volcanic strength, the kind that erupts dazzlingly, heaving boulders the size of hovels hundreds of yards. Its display is awesome and lets the opponents question their own strength. The explosive power of Michael made the rounds of the cantina and piazzas, as each listener added one more pound to the cumbersome load, or one more inch to the foe's stature. Michael's might was indeed awesome and well-broadcasted in his region.

Salvatore's strength combined the long, angular muscles of his arms and back to mental toughness which was invincible.

The faces of the spectators revealed a basic doubt: Would brute force overcome the steady application of a determined spirit? It was almost an animal versus man confrontation.

Even Michael and Salvatore sensed that there was something special about this arm joust. Michael had never lost an arm wrestling contest in his life. But Salvatore's challenge sent a slight twinge of fear into the pit of his stomach. Salvatore couldn't believe he voiced the challenge, but realized that he could not back out now.

Salvatore and Michael lay on their stomachs, both resting on their right elbows. Cangeliera acted as official - a biased one, as he hoped for Michael's defeat. Michael made an abrupt attempt to commence the duel before the official start was given but Salvatore protested that he was caught off guard. Some money passed hands as modest wagers were made among the pack.

"Are you ready now?" jeered Michael.

"Yes, I have a chance now to beat you."

No advantage was gained the first couple of moments. Michael acted as though he were toying with Salvatore. Salvatore fought off the powerful onslaught. His was clearly a defensive maneuver.

Never could Salvatore marshal an offensive. Yet Michael had never felt such vibrancy in the arms of any of his other vanquished opponents. Salvatore had found a balanced resistance to the kinetic might of his powerful brother-in-law. No fatigue or ache. Michael's face showed greater strain. As Salvatore phrased a conciliatory statement to call it a stalemate, a gunshot startled the group. Whirling in his tracks, Cangeliera spotted a group of twenty Gendarmes riding up the rear side of the hill.

Shots were ricocheting around the impromptu campsite. One hit and severed the vertical limb of the spit, spilling the sacrificial pig into the embers.

The only safe escape was toward the tall wheat fields several hundred yards away. The men seized what weapons they could. The horses and mules were lead to the tall wheat sanctuary. Luckily, the firing was inaccurate, since the Carabinieri were shooting and riding at top speed.

Spilatieri ran with Bellaria to his old horse. Bellaria and Spilatieri had been riding double, since Spilatieri owned no horse of his own when he joined the clan. Bellaria kicked the horse viciously on the flank to generate more speed from the basically lazy steed. These commandeered work horses were no match for the fine, speedy horses of the federal police.

The duo fell behind their comrades in their frantic escape to the tall grasses. The horse rebelled at the wrong time and stopped abruptly for no apparent reason. Bellaria was thrown over the horse's huge head.

His fall was broken when he hit a short wide bush. Bellaria glanced back at Spilatieri. He was shaking his head, obviously stunned by the fall. Bellaria called repeatedly for Spilatieri to beat it into the grassy area. Spilatieri remained motionless. He stumbled and fell back to the ground. Bellaria judged the Gendarmes to be five hundred yards away. Finally, Spilatieri realized what was happening and lunged awkwardly toward Bellaria. Bellaria felt easier now that he was ambulatory and beating it toward safety. He then ran frantically to catch up with Salvatore and Michael.

The Gendarmes raced wildly when they saw the laggard Spilatieri. One captured brigand was needed to shed some light on this new criminal enterprise arising in their district.

The lead mount knew that once the peasant figure reached the grass, the chase would be over. He wanted his fugitive alive. Spilatieri felt his lungs about to burst for want of oxygen. When he tried to sneak a quick glance over his shoulder to see his pursuers, he tripped over a boulder the earth had spit out from its bowels to rest on the surface. Spilatieri made no effort to resume his retreat. He remained with his face in the arid, Sicilian earth and felt the ground reverberate with the rapid thuds of galloping horses. Before he could stand up, four Gendarmes on horses had surrounded him pointing their rifles at him.

Meanwhile, the others were rapidly moving away from the hill fairly well protected by the tall weeds. Having seen Spilatieri's capture, Salvatore hoped that on their return trip that they could rescue him. Any attempt to rescue him now was out of the question. Such a futile attempt would probably cost all their lives. They must wait.

A lieutenant rode up to the captors of Spilatieri and ordered the frightened captive on a horse. As quickly as they had come, they left, probably realizing that a search for the others would be futile and highly risky.

After nearly an hour of waiting, the men assembled still under their natural cover. Michael was the first to speak.

"We must move on quickly in case they come back. We'll try to rescue him on our way back. It's the only way. Let's go!"

The group quickly mounted their horses and galloped towards the Delvecchio estate in the Malpasso country side. Michael wondered what would happen to Spilatieri.

Spilatieri was tossed hard into a cell with no windows and lit only by a weak light in the far corner. The luminosity fluctuated with the unsteady source of power. In the middle of the room was a desk with two chairs. The walls were stark bare. Except for a small bench against the wall opposite the entrance, the room was empty. The room had heard and seen much.

Lieutenant Pavesi pulled a chair around the table so that he could face the other chair. Pointing to the other chair, Pavesi told Spilatieri to sit down. A guard locked the door from the inside and sat down on the bench.

"Well, well, what have we here?" asked the perfectly groomed Pavesi. "Tell me desperado, who else rides in your gang?"

Spilatieri didn't answer. Silence spread across the room for a few moments. Suddenly, Pavesi picked up his shiny black cane and slammed it against the table. The thunder-bolt clap alarmed Pavesi more than it did Spilatieri.

"I asked you a question!"

Spilatieri, now trembled, but remained silent.

"Look at you, you shake like a woman. You are going to talk, do you understand? You filthy Sicilian scum!"

Spilatieri looked at the young Lieutenant, then he spit on the ground.

Bursting out laughing, the officer jumped to his feet.

"Very good, son of a whore. I'll call you asshole because I don't know your name and, mainly, because all Sicilians are assholes, bastards."

Giving Spilatieri a crazed look, the Lieutenant continued. "Go ahead, asshole. Spit on the ground again. I dare you. Italy dares you to spit on the ground, you Sicilian son of a whore!"

Calmly, Spilatieri spit on the officer. The spittle dripped from his cheek. Two strong hands grabbed the petrified Spilatieri from behind as Pavesi approached him. Tediously pulling out his handkerchief, Pavesi wiped the spit from his face. He then picked up his cane and jammed it hard into Spilatieri's groin.

Screaming wildly, Spilatieri insulted Pavesi by saying that his mother fornicated with horses.

"You son of a ..." screamed Pavesi as he batted his victim's head with his came. "Listen, I'm going to kill you if you don't tell me what I want to know. Do you understand? I promise I'll let you go if you tell me the truth."

Spilatieri laughed hysterically. Pavesi, thinking he was psychologically in tune with his victim, laughed along with him.

"I'll give you my word on an Italian officer," declared Pavesi.

"To the devil with you and Italy! I'm Sicilian, not Italian." screamed Spilatieri.

That was the last statement Spilatieri remembered saying before he lost consciousness.

It seemed that he had been out for weeks, but it had obviously been only a matter of minutes. The warmth of the gushing blood from his nose and mouth greeted Spilatieri as he slowly regained his senses. His vision, still rather blurred, impaired him from seeing the lieutenant clearly, but he could make out his voice distinctly.

After several minutes of dizziness, he finally was able to sit up. He touched his nose and mouth only to realize that they were both shattered. The incredible amounts of blood were beginning to sicken him. Spilatieri knew that he wouldn't live to see the morning. Whether he talked or not, these Gendarmes were going to kill him. His only escape from dying like a dog was to infuriate the rash young officer to such a point that he would shoot him to end the pain and the blood.

Feeling that he was about to throw up, Spilatieri mustered all the energy he could and lunged towards the beautiful, perfectly kept uniform. Spewing vomit all over the horrified Pavesi's uniform, Spilatieri attempted to laugh, but couldn't as he was violently thrown to the ground.

Screaming, the outraged Pavesi ordered the guard not to touch Spilatieri as he stormed out of the cell. Squirming on his stomach, Spilatieri was finally able to turn over on his back. Propping his body on his elbows, he looked over to the guard.

"Shoot me," he begged. "Please shoot me. You are Sicilian; didn't you hear what he said?"

The guard, sympathetic, attempted to speak but was interrupted by Pavesi's entrance into the room.

"Sit him on the bench. No, better yet, lie him down on the desk here. I'm going to make him talk if it's the last thing I do!" yelled Pavesi.

With some difficulty, the guard managed to drag Spilatieri's body onto the table. Pavesi paced the floor for several minutes. Of course, Pavesi had figured out his prisoner's game and was rather upset that he had fallen into Spilatieri' s trap. He must not hurt him too much, just enough to let him know that the pain would go on.

This man must be part of the granary robbery. He could wait to confirm the fact, but Pavesi wanted to impress the Colonel. His promotion was due anytime; if he caught his gang of petty thieves, he thought, he could get promoted. As a captain he could ask for Marina Delvecchio's hand. The old man would be back in a week. Pavesi could be Captain Pavesi by then. Marina Pavesi had a nice ring to it, thought Pavesi. Marina Pavesi.

Turning his back on Spilatieri, Pavesi closed his eyes and tried to concentrate on the matter at hand. What would make this man talk?

Meanwhile, the guard gestured for Spilatieri to grab his gun at some opportune time. Spilatieri immediately understood and blew a kiss in the guard's direction.

Turning around, Pavesi smiled at Spilatieri.

"All right, if you want to play games, we shall. If you don't talk to me tonight, right now, I shall go home. We will wait until you are identified and then you and I and some of my lonely men shall go visit your family. You are married, are you not? Maybe you have a young daughter. We shall see whose ass gets fucked!"

"You wouldn't," screamed Spilatieri as he grabbed for the guard's gun. Struggling with Spilatieri, the guard pointed the gun at his head and pulled the trigger.

Giuseppe Spilatieri fell instantly dead. Pavesi would have to wait on the promotion, at least for now.

The marauding band was now some twenty feet away from the main entrance of the Delvecchio estate. Signaling for the men to spread out and surround the area, Salvatore, Bellaria, and Cangeliera took their rifles off their backs and proceeded cautiously towards the front door.

Knocking loudly on the door, Salvatore waited for several minutes until he heard a male voice questioning his identity.

"We are here to see the Baron," lied Salvatore knowing that Delvecchio was not at home.

Opening the door, an elderly servant in the midst of explaining the Baron's absence was greeted with three rifles pointed at his head. Stepping slowly backwards, the servant, followed by the bandits, moved to the center of the room.

"Who was it?" asked a beautiful, elegant lady as she walked into the living room. Shocked by the presence of the three armed men, the trembling wife of the Baron asked the intruders what it was that they wanted.

"You!" laughed Cangeliera whose incessant glaring at the lady of the house caused some concern in Salvatore's mind.

"Shut up!" snapped Salvatore to Cangeliera. "We mean no harm to you dear lady. We are poor, hungry men who have families. All we ask is enough food and money to sustain us. We will be on our way very soon."

Nodding fearfully, she walked over to the panic-stricken servant and whispered to him to go and stay with the children. Quickly, she walked across the room towards a large portrait of herself. Removing the portrait from the wall, she uncovered a safe which she presently opened. Pulling out a small jewelry sack, she closed the safe and walked calmly back to a table in the center of the parlor. Dumping nearly thirty thousand lire in currency on the table, she muttered:

"Is this enough?"

"Yes," began Cangeliera.

"No, no. It's too much." interjected Salvatore staring hard at Cangeliera and then added, "We will take only a third of this, Signora."

Nodding, she pointed to a door.

"The storage area is over there. There is plenty of food. Take what you want but please, leave immediately."

"Thank you. Thank you. We will be gone in a few moments," responded Salvatore.

"Why don't we take it all?" exclaimed Cangeliera, eyeing the remainder of the money still scattered over the table.

"Because we don't need it! Let's go now."

Swearing under his breath, Cangeliera gazed at the lady of the house and made an obscene gesture with his tongue which went unnoticed by Salvatore and Bellaria.

At that moment Michael walked in the door.

"Jesus, what a beautiful woman!" he exclaimed to Salvatore dismay.

"Come on. Let's go!" yelled Salvatore to the men who quickly followed him out of the house towards the storage area.

"Why did you have to say such a thing?" he said angrily to Michael. "The woman is alone and frightened enough without all you assholes looking like you are about to jump on her."

"Oh, stop it. I was just paying her a compliment! You are so frightened of everything," responded Michael.

"Alright. Forget it. We have work to do. Call the others and have them bring their horses over to the storage area so that we can easily load the horses."

Waiting impatiently by the entrance of the storage area, Salvatore and Cangeliera stood silently for about ten minutes. Salvatore was beginning to worry more and more about Cangeliera. First he had wanted to shoot the boys who had spied on them, now he wanted to take more than he needed. Fearing that the members of the band may become criminals not for the need to feed their families, but for their own personal gain, wouldn't ever be a problem, but Cangeliera had to be watched. The ex-supervisor still had a good deal of influence over the men. It was becoming a tricky situation; Salvatore truly hoped that the group wouldn't become uncontrollable.

Finally, Michael appeared pulling his horse. He was followed by the remaining members of the gang. Salvatore entered the storage area and began searching for worthwhile goods to take. Nearly an hour passed, as the men, working as quickly as possible, loaded their horses. After having looked about to see if everyone was ready, Salvatore mounted his horse and ordered the group to ready themselves.

"Let's head for the woods," said Cangeliera a bit annoyed at Salvatore's growing importance as a leader of the gang.

"We will stay there for a few days and spy on this place to see what the Gendarmes do."

Agreeing, the men mounted and headed for the woods. A much-relieved Baroness Delvecchio stared out the window hoping she would never see them again. She would.

The gang spent a few days in the woods planning various strategies and keeping the Delvecchio estate under constant surveillance. Using binoculars, and taking six-hour shifts, the gang watched the estate on a twenty-four hour basis.

Delvecchio came back home the next day, much earlier than expected. A regiment of Gendarmes stopped by the estate, only to leave several hours later. Of interesting note was the regular presence of a young officer. Carmine Bellaria was the first one to notice him. Every day the officer would walk with a girl, probably Delvecchio's daughter from his first wife. Actually from their view, the daughter looked about the same age as the wife. There were only six years separating the two.

A few days passed quickly for most, but not for Michael who was to meet his wife and children at

Tramontane's at the end of this waiting period. Finally, his excitement reaching incredible heights, Michael was sent off by the gang with their blessings and their funds. Rosalia was to distribute the money among the families of the fugitives. Michael was to see Rosalia that night. He was wild with anticipation.

During the time that Michael was going to meet Rosalia, the gang planned and executed two more robberies, always taking only what they needed. Their first visit was to the residence of the Marquis Bettina who lived in Alimena, about twenty-five kilometers north of Villarosa. Then, in Rosattana, located three kilometers north of Alimena, the gang visited and successfully extracted some funds from Cavalieri Zanguri. The gang was able to make these two stops and then return to the woods near Delvecchio's in order to await Michael's return.

Rosalia Moccia opened the door and welcomed Tramontane's hired hand into her house. Tramontane had sent Pasquale to aid Rosalia and the children in the journey to meet her husband. Placing some wine and pasta on the table, she invited Pasquale to eat something before they left. Graciously accepting the offer, Pasquale sat down at the table and began eating while Rosalia made last minute preparations to make the trip.

Wearing clothes that would disguise her, she placed the two small children in baskets on the mule, and proceeded, with Pasquale, slowly out of Villarosa towards Tramontane's farm. Travelling in late afternoon, the small group arrived at the Sasso River by early evening.

Pasquale heard the roar of the angry river several miles before reaching it. Rain water rolled off the baked Sicilian landscape quickly. Little precious water seeped into the parched earth. The Sasso River usually presented no problem to travelers. Fording places were numerous and safe. Mothers permitted fidgety boys to romp crazily in the river most of the spring and summer. The Sasso emitted a unique sound when it served as the conduit for the entire valley after a violent summer thunder storm, a sound similar to a freight train speeding with several cars off the track. Astute villagers could predict the river's height by the intensity of the rumbling sound. On the day Rosalia travelled to see her beloved husband the river noise equaled the train yards of Palermo in volume and intensity. Rosalia and Pasquale both grew apprehensive as they descended the gradual terrain toward the river bed itself.

The children grew tired sealed up in strong, wicker orchard baskets, the light yellow container bobbed rhythmically, secured to the strong back of the trusty mule. Rosalia reassured them that they were getting closer and that their release from the wicker coffins was imminent. The children sensed this was no game they were playing with their mother and escort. They gave adult cooperation since they reasoned that their father's well-being was connected with this strange pilgrimage in the night.

Pasquale's eyes searched the turgid waters for a safe ford. He tested familiar spots himself by wading cautiously into the churning flow of muddy water. Quickly, the water would exceed his five-foot stature, and Pasquale would retreat exhausted to the trio and beast whose safety was his responsibility.

A dilemma posed itself to this simple peasant: "What the hell am I to do?"

Rendezvous time was set. Tardiness could not be tolerated when things were developing so speedily. Yet he too knew the great rage of which Michael was capable should Michael's family encounter misfortune or tragedy under his supervision.

Rosalia was anxious to be reunited with Michael. The two kids could not remain encased much longer. At a sharp bend in the river's trajectory, Pasquale found that he could wade almost to the center and remain above water. The wider expanse at this point lowered the depth and kept it fairly constant.

They rested and steeled themselves to challenge the Sasso at the penetrable spot. Rosalia allowed the children to pop out of the baskets for some air and movement. They stared at the frightening river and stood silent in awe and fear. Rosalia sensed their great fear and quickly intervened to restore their slipping bravery.

"Poppa is on the other side. You must not move in the baskets or startle the mule. You might get a little wet when the water enters the holes but we will remove the coverings from your heads so you have more room to stretch your necks above the water."

The children trusted Rosalia's assessment of things blindly. Her advice had never failed them. Mamma knew all things, especially when it came to what might hurt her flesh and blood.

With the mule in the middle, Rosalia on one side to guide Clara in her basket and Pasquale on the other side to vouchsafe Gino, the timorous group of mule, children, and guardians left the sure-footedness of the bank to traverse thirty yards of hostile element to keep a promise to a man eager to kiss and embrace the only things in life he loved.

There was no turning back, for to risk a tricky about-face maneuver at mid-stream would subject the amphibious quintet to certain peril Rosalia prayed visibly, with her thin lips forming every syllable distinctly. The river bed contained stones and boulders, rounded out by the eternal passage of rapid water over their granite surface. One could feel for sharp impediments in one's path and circumvent them. The larger rounded stones could deceive, however. Before the usually sure-footed beast sensed it, his four feet rested on one of the rounders. No foot remained fixed on the traction of sand and loose gravel; all four props rested on slippery, mossy rocks. The mule lunged forward to get the feel of something softer under his feet.

Suddenly, as water entered the baskets, the children let out a loud scream. Frightened, the mule took a step backwards which caused the animal to stumble and fall on its side. Rosalia, seeing that the mule was about to fall, attempted to grab the basket closest to her, but the mule fell on top of her, pinning her under the cold rushing currents. Pasquale, desperately trying to yank the mule off Rosalia, didn't notice that the baskets had freed themselves from the mule's back. For nearly five agonizing minutes, Pasquale tried to pull Rosalia from under the weight of the mule, when suddenly the mule, able to get up, raced for the shore. Dragging the lifeless Rosalia to the shore, Pasquale raced back into the dark waters to search for the children.

Up until midnight Pasquale, with the help of some farmers, searched the river for the children; after midnight word had gotten out to all the farmers along the river about the accident. After midnight the searching party almost tripled as caring and kind farmers in the vicinity joined in on the search for the children. They found the children dead naked on a rock just a few moments after sunrise.

When Tramontane saw the mule with Rosalia's body tied to it, he raced out of his house. A crying Pasquale explained the horrible details; Tramontane has his wife broke down into fits of despair.

Realizing that Michael was arriving that night, Tramontane decided to take the corpses to Villarosa for a decent burial. He would leave before Michael's arrival; he didn't want Michael to see his battered family and that funeral had to take place without Michael's presence, since he was an outlaw. Tramontane would have to invent some story for the authorities.

I'm going to take Pasquale with me," said Tramontane to his wife. "He will be needed as a witness. I shall be back the day after tomorrow. Will you be all right?"

Nodding, the crying Maria thought about how she would tell Michael. She had always kidded him; she had never been serious with him.

And now, she was to tell him that his world was dead. His best friend, his wife and his children all had died in a period of less than two months, she thought. What would keep him from wanting to die himself? She wished Salvatore would be there, but she would have to deal with the situation alone.

Her empty house seemed unfriendly to her as she anxiously waited for Michael's arrival. Splashing water on her face to refresh herself and awaken her to the morbid task before her, she heard the loud excitement knock on the door. Her heart stopped as she turned towards the door.

For what seemed an eternity she stood behind, the door attempting to muster enough courage to open the door to the smiling Michael.

Michael's excited smile evaporated instantly as he looked into Maria's eyes. The beautiful woman, looking more striking than ever, was standing in front of him nervously clasping her hands. Her eyes, though, revealed tremendous sorrow not only because they had obviously been crying for hours, but because that high voltage spark of wit, of life that usually pervaded those magnificent blue orbs was gone. Instead, there was a horrible void in her stare, a void that frightened Michael more than he had ever been frightened in his life.

Suddenly, she lunged at him. Wrapping her arms around his neck she clasped his body with hers so tightly that Michael lost his breath. Sobbing, kissing him on the neck, her mad greeting excited the panic-stricken Michael. Trembling with fear, Michael thought that something horrible must have happened to her husband for he was nowhere in sight; nor were Rosalia and the children for that matter.

Kissing her softly on the head, he asked, "Where is your husband? What happened to him?"

She replied by increasing her crying, having revealed that Michael had assumed that the loss was hers rather than his. Removing her arms from around his neck, Maria grabbed both of his hands and pulled him to the couch. Once seated, she began caressing his face and sobbing hysterically.

Totally confused by her demonstration of affection yet knowing that he must try and help her, he grabbed her hands and implored her to calm herself.

"Please," whispered Michael. "Calm down and tell me what happened. Please."

"Michael," she sobbed. "Oh Michael, it's Rosalia. They are dead."

Color drained out of his face. Maria stopped crying and held on to Michael, staring into his lifeless eyes. Michael began to breathe deeply as he continued to look into her eyes for stability. His mind, his body wanted to explode into screams; his total being was shocked to a point of no return.

"Dead?" he asked in a voice that questioned its own existence.

"Dead!"

As he jumped up, she pushed him back down on the couch.

"Don't move Michael. Don't you do anything stupid.

Please let me stay with you! Don't move."

Bursting into fits of crying, he grabbed Maria and held her as if he were holding on for life. Her presence, her warmth next to him had become his only contact with reality. Fearing he would lose his sanity, Michael held her on top of him as he cried spasmodically.

Screaming evolved from his crying. Kissing him, trying desperately to calm his state of tumultuous agitation, she began to pray that he wouldn't lose his mind. His moods seemed to jump from self-pity to bitter hatred for the world and she seemed to be the only tangible thing that his destroyed, paranoid psyche could trust.

As he was running his fingers through her long, golden hair, he pulled her face closer to his and began kissing her on the lips. His entire body reacted as if it were trying to inhale all the warmth, all the life from her body.

'Michael," she continued sobbing as his hands moved to the back of her blouse. Yanking from the neck downwards, he ripped Maria's blouse off her back. Gasping, she, realizing that nothing could stop Michael, was drawn into his desperation, his urgent need for her. Passionately she responded to his kisses as he continued tearing her garments off of her body.

The entire night he clung to her, repeatedly attempting to drown his sorrows in a sensual rapport with Maria. The long hours, combined with wine and the physical exhaustion seemed to drain Michael's energy as well as to cool the fiery pain in his soul.

Morning found the pair sound asleep on the parlor floor. The front door, still ajar from the previous evening, was swinging lightly under the influence of a light breeze. Sharp morning weather infiltrated the room and startled Maria. Slowly stretching, she stood up and quickly ran to the door and closed it. Walking to the bedroom, she grabbed some blankets and returned to cover Michael.

Heading towards her room with her torn clothes in her hand, her mind was a cobweb of confusion. Her sincere sorrow for Michael's misfortune was heavily weighed against the fact that she admittedly was content about the events that had taken place between Michael and her. Never had anyone been so passionate with her. It was useless to imagine that she did it for him. Possibly this was a consideration, but she had wanted him for a long time and last night had proven a perfect opportunity. The guilt that she felt was not due to her actions, but to the fact that she was becoming less and less hurt about Michael's tragedies.

She hurried over to the stove and threw her torn clothes into the fire. She slowly, meticulously dressed herself as she attempted to remove the thoughts about Michael from her mind.

Pondering over the events of the night, Maria re-entered the parlor to ask Michael if he were hungry. Michael was gone.

Michael felt the blanket drop on his naked body. Hearing her footsteps drop off in the distance, he got up and began to dress himself. Not knowing what to say to her, he quickly decided to leave. Michael was totally drained emotionally as well as physically. He quickly decided to leave. He quietly opened the door and left the Tramontane house. He took the reins of his horse into his weak grip, and walked the horse for several hundred yards so as not to be overheard. Safely away from the farm house, he galloped away from the memories, both heart-rending and beautiful. The cold early morning weather pinched his face. Before he rejoined Salvatore, he headed south to the cemetery where he disguised himself and was able to see the graves of his loved ones.

For hours he would count the trees, the clouds, anything that would inhibit him from thinking about Maria. His wife and children had just died, he thought, and all he could do was think about Maria. She had become part of him, had understood his pain, his passion, his need for her. Maria filled the immense void that death had carved out. Michael couldn't comprehend this strange dual love in him, deep pure love for his good, loyal wife; hot, overpowering sensuality for that great blonde beauty, Maria. Why could not one woman generate that exotic blend?

Not resting, Michael rode all morning and entered the woods by Delvecchio's estate around noon. After nearly an hour, he spotted the group camped on the side of the small hill. As he approached the group, he saw Salvatore jump to his feet and walked out to meet him.

Salvatore couldn't believe his eyes when he saw Michael riding up towards the small encampment. Concerned, he began to walk towards Michael wondering what had gone wrong.

"What are you doing here?" questioned Salvatore as Michael came into earshot. He didn't answer; he just stopped his horse and dismounted. Pulling out the money that was supposed to be given to Rosalia, he re-marked blandly, "I forgot."

"What happened?" asked Salvatore following Michael into the camp.

"There was an accident. My family is dead," said Michael with frightening calm. "Everyone is lost. My life is finished-"

Shocked, Salvatore grabbed Michael's arm.

"Michael, I ... how-"

"No more words. Words only put the hurt deeper into my stomach. We can discuss it later, what there is to discuss."

Walking slowly towards the fire, Michael gathered some bread, wine and a piece of rancid cheese and sat himself down away from the group. The most terrifying aspect to Salvatore was Michael's reaction. If he were crying or screaming, it would have made sense, but this, this total nonchalance was incredible.

"How are we going to get the money to our fami-lies?" asked Cangeliera.

"I'll take it in two weeks," answered Michael. "That way I'll be able to visit the cemetery again."

Possibly the shock had been too much for him, thought Salvatore. After all, Franco had died, then his entire family. How atrocious!

Tears in his eyes, Salvatore walked to Michael and sat next to him. Wondering what he would say to him, he merely looked at his friend who was deeply concentrat-ing on his food.

"I cried last night. I have nothing left, no soul, no

heart, no emotions," said Michael softly after a prolonged silence.

"I ... I cried before I made love to Maria." he said emphatically as he turned to look at Salvatore. "Can you believe it? I cried over my wife's death and then made love to another woman!"

"Listen, I'm sure it wasn't like that. You needed- I don't even care, that's what scares me. I don't care about what I did with Maria. In fact, if I want to be honest with myself, I must admit that I have been thinking more of her than of Rosalia. What devil lives within me? Am I Satan?"

"That's natural. There's nothing wrong with what you did. Who can judge what a man does when great tragedy strikes?"

"Always see the good side of things, don't you Salvatore? I could kill a hundred babies and you would see something good in that, wouldn't you? Don't you realize that I'm no good, that something vile uses my body for its home?"

"You didn't kill anybody, though, did you?" said Salvatore harshly. "Maria was there at the time and she helped you with your pain. Rosalia would have wanted it that way-"

"Rosalia? Oh yes, look how I've disgraced her. I get drunk and make love with a beautiful lady on the day that she dies. Such tremendous respect I showed!" yelled Michael. "I would have no trouble killing any man who showed that great dishonor to my sister, even you. You sit there and forgive all. What must I do to prove my rottenness to you, my brother?"

"No, quit being a fool! Listen to me, Michael. Disrespect would be the case only if you had done what you did on purpose, not out of despair or some incredible need to forget your pain. You were a man out of control."

"I don't want to talk about it!" yelled Michael at Salvatore, who stood up and walked away.

For two days the friends didn't speak to each other; Michael ate and slept by himself. During the day, he would walk around the woods attempting to resolve his conflicts. At night, he would suffer from horrid nightmares that often awoke the entire group. The same nightmare—wolves ripping the flesh of his family while he watched paralyzed.

Slowly, as the week went by, he would say a few words to Salvatore. On the eighth day after his arrival, as he was about to take his daily walk, he motioned for Salvatore to accompany him.

"I'm sorry," he said when Salvatore was by his side.

"Forget it. How do you feel?" asked Salvatore eagerly.

"Either you are right or what you said is what I want to believe. I don't know which, neither do I care. One can suffer only so much. You know what I mean?" said Michael as he punched Salvatore in the arm and ran away laughing.

"You son of a bitch," laughed Salvatore as he chased him into the woods.

Speaking of the events that had taken place in their lives in the last few months, Salvatore and Michael spent many hours in those woods. If it had not been for the others grumbling about staying there, they would have remained in the area for weeks.

"So what are we going to do now?" asked Cangeliera in the direction of Salvatore and Michael.

"I think we should get some more money so that we can give our families large, chunks at a time. That way we don't have to expose them to danger so often," stated Bellaria.

Agreeing, Cangeliera pointed out that Delvecchio could stand another visit, especially since the baron was now at home. Salvatore didn't think the idea bad, so, after dinner, the men decided to visit the baron.

Putting out the fire, the men collected all their belongings and mounted their horses. Quietly, under the cover of night, they rode within four hundred yards of the estate. Dismounting, they left the horses under the supervision of Carmine Bellaria. Proceeding slowly towards the house, the men spread out around the house.

Salvatore, Michael, and Cangeliera walked towards the front door which was strangely slightly ajar. Cangeliera suspected a trick when he saw the open door — an invitation to death. Quickly opening a door, Michael walked into the house. The baron was sitting at his desk looking over some papers, while his wife was reading at the table. Startled, the baron jumped to his feet.

"Don't move or I'll scatter your brains across the wall." yelled Michael.

Cangeliera walked over to the wife and motioned for her to get up.

"Pleased to see me again, aren't you?" he whispered to her.

Terrified she ran over to her husband. Michael and Salvatore went about the house looking for the others. Meanwhile, the baron was whispering something to his wife, looking at Cangeliera.

"My wife tells me that you are interested in money? More so than others, perhaps?" mused Delvecchio.

"Perhaps," answered Cangeliera.

"Why don't you meet me here in two days? Maybe we can work out a deal?"

"What do you think, I'm stupid? What would stop you from killing me?"

"Just the fact that I have a wife and several children should be enough insurance for you. Do you know what I mean? One of your friends could easily kill them if anything happened to you. Think about it! It could mean one hundred thousand lire for you."

As he heard the sum, Cangeliera's eyes lit up.

"I'll bring a friend, though," he said cautiously.

"Fine. In two days at noon. One hundred-"

The baron stopped as he saw Michael walk into the room with the Delvecchio children and two servants.

"This is it," said Michael pointing to the new additions to the room. "I can't find anyone else."

Salvatore, entering the room, acknowledged Michael's find and proceeded towards the baron.

"Baron Delvecchio, we are interested in a small sum of money to sustain our families and-"

"You disgusting thieves. Wait until the Gendarmes

get a hold of you. You will end up dead just like that poor son of a-"

"You mean he's dead," screamed Michael speaking of Spilatieri.

"Of course he is!"

Grabbing Marina Delvecchio, the baron's twenty year old daughter, Michael walked the trembling girl over to the baron's side.

"Who did it?" he screamed. "Who killed him?"

"How should I know?"

"You see your daughter?" yelled Michael, putting his rifle against her temple. "How would you like to see her after all these men have had fun with her? You have ten seconds to answer me. Who did it?"

"Lieutenant Pavesi," screamed the frightened girl's step mother.

"Thank you," said Michael as he walked the girl back to her brothers.

"I'm sorry, but a man's daughter is always his prize possession. I wouldn't have done anything, truly," Michael snickered.

"All right Baron Delvecchio, we must be on our way soon. Please offer us ten thousand lire and we will be on our way." said Salvatore.

"Surely," he smiled as he placed the money on the table and then added, "You must try some of my new bread. It was just made today."

Thanking him, Salvatore gathered up the money while Michael gathered some loaves of bread. Quickly, the men left the house. Cangeliera, the last one out, put two fingers up in the air to make the baron understand that he would indeed be at the meetings. Michael had made himself an enemy of Delvecchio, thought Cangeliera. Thinking that he was going to make sure that Delvecchio was going to hate Michael, Cangeliera glanced at Delvecchio's daughter. Walking out the door, he smiled, knowing that he had found a way to avenge himself for the twofold humiliation he suffered at the hands of Michael Moccia, in the mines and before the spying youth.

The group rode for about an hour before deciding that it was safe to stop. A shepherd and his flock of sheep were passing by. Michael mused how sweet it would be to be a herder of sheep. Peace and tranquility doing useful work - a gift of a job. His new existence, alone and a bandit, was far from peaceful. Things were changing too fast for any good to come from them.

Dismounting, Carmine Bellaria began to construct a fire as Michael pulled out some of Delvecchio's bread. As he was about to take a bite into a loaf, Salvatore screamed.

Why would that skunk Delvecchio offer bread to men robbing him if not to poison their guts? "Wait! Wait a minute, let me see that bread. I don't like the way he offered it to us."

Ripping the bread open, he began to thoroughly check it.

"I can't see or smell anything, but I think it's poisoned," stated Salvatore.

Taking a small piece of bread, he put it on the ground

near where a sheep was drinking. Noticing the bread, the sheep cautiously moved towards it, then began to chew it. Not even two minutes later, the sheep went into convulsions and died. Horrified, Michael vowed that he would kill the baron.

"What did you say?" asked Cangeliera.

"I said I'm going to fuck his daughter in the ass," repeated Michael as a manner of speech. Perfect, thought Cangeliera. Just perfect.

Throwing the poisonous bread away, the men ate some of their remaining food. Salvatore did not forget to pay the shepherd a fair amount for the loss of the sheep.

"We'll take nothing from peasants."

After several discussions on what their next move would be, the men retired.

Stefano Cangeliera waited until past midnight. Quietly rising, he dressed himself quickly and went to his horse. Walking his horse until out of audible range, he silently mounted and headed for the Delvecchio estate. Betting that the old man had gone for help, Cangeliera knew he had to move quickly. When he arrived at the gate, he tied his horse and walked cautiously towards the house.

There was a woman in the parlor, but Cangeliera couldn't make out whether it was the mother or the daughter. Crawling under the window by the door, Cangeliera threw a pebble at the door and waited.

Oreste?" questioned the woman. "Oreste Pavesi what are you doing?" giggled the woman as she stepped out of the door. Immediately recognizing the daughter's voice,

Cangeliera's heart began pounding. Absolutely perfect, be thought.

By the time he returned to the camp, it was nearly dawn. As silently as he had left, Cangeliera slithered back into the camp. Once bedded down again, he leaned over to Santo Bellaria and shook his friend.

"Santo, wake up. Come on, get up now," whispered Cangeliera

"What ... what's going on?" mumbled the sleepy Bellaria.

Listen, wake up. I have something important to tell you. Wake up damn you!" said Cangeliera angrily.

"What's so important?" asked Bellaria as he rubbed his eyes and propped his body upon his elbows.

"Listen carefully. When we were inside the house tonight, the old man asked me to come to see him in two days. He said that we could make a hundred thousand lire!"

"Wait a minute, where do you get we?" questioned the baffled Bellaria.

"I told him about you," said Cangeliera, holding up his head thereby indicating that he didn't want to be interrupted. "One hundred thousand lire?"

"How can you trust him after he tried to poison us?" asked Bellaria. "How can you be so stupid?"

"Listen to me idiot!" said Cangeliera, visibly angry. "The baron has a beautiful wife, two sons, and a large beautiful estate. He has a lot to lose. We will make him think of that if we don't come back."

"Yeah!" exclaimed Bellaria excited. "You forgot

about his daughter."

"Huh?"

"His daughter. He has a daughter, too. Don't you remember?"

"Oh yes, of course. The one Moccia said he was going to-"

"Yes, her," laughed Bellaria. "When are we to meet him?"

"Tomorrow," said Cangeliera.

"Yes, I know but when and where?"

"At noon at his house.

CHAPTER **SEVEN**

LIEUTENANT CRESTS PAVESI paced the floor of the Delvecchio parlor. Gloves in hand, he was slapping the gloves against his right leg as he continued pacing the length of the room.

"Will you please sit down!" exclaimed a weary, irritated Baron Delvecchio.

Whirling about to face the baron, Pavesi muttered apologetically as he headed for the nearest chair. Sitting next to the exhausted baroness, Pavesi looked up at the clock to see that it was nearly noon. Marina was out of danger. Her condition was becoming stable, but she was still in shock. Pavesi swore under his breath.

The house had been a chaotic to-and-fro of Gendarmes and doctors. Baron Delvecchio, showing real signs of fatigue, hadn't slept in over seventy-two hours, neither had anyone else.

Delvecchio had immediately gone to summon Pavesi the night that the bandits had come. After two hours of fast travelling, he had arrived at the post, where he had found Pavesi asleep. Waking him, he ordered Pavesi to get some men to go protect his house. Delvecchio could order Pavesi not only because of his noble ranking, but mainly because Pavesi was in love with Marina.

Dutifully, Pavesi had amassed twenty men and, along

with the baron, commenced the journey back to the estate.

"Oreste, we must hurry. I poisoned the bread that they stole. They will most certainly come back."

"Sir, if I may say so, that wasn't a wise idea. These peasants can be ruthless."

"I'm not interested in your opinion, just let's get moving!"

From quite a distance, Pavesi had noticed that all the lights were on in the house. Pointing out this fact to Delvecchio made the old man unbelievable anxious.

The men began to move at maximum speed. Nearly twenty minutes later, the wheezing horses pulled up by the estate. Delvecchio was greeted by his frantic wife screaming something incomprehensible about Marina.

"Where is she?" asked Pavesi panic-stricken.

"I don't know, she was here, then gone, not even an hour ago," cried the baroness.

"Spread out in a big circle and move outwards until you find her!" barked Pavesi to his men.

For hours, everyone searched the area for Marina. Becoming desperate, Delvecchio began insulting Pavesi for being unable to find his daughter. Then Pavesi spotted her.

Ordering his men to go back to the house, the trembling Pavesi and Delvecchio approached Marina. She was lying on her back, with her arms tied above her around a tree. Completely naked, her bloodstained face and body was a witness to a horrible rape. Thinking her dead, Pavesi slowly dismounted from his horse and fell to his knees weeping. Delvecchio immediately went to her side and put his ear to her chest to check for a heartbeat.

"She's alive!" he screamed as he frantically tried to untie her hands.

Pavesi ran to Delvecchio's side, pulled out his sword and cut her loose. Taking his coat off, the crying father wrapped his daughter in it, and then the two men cautiously put her on Pavesi's horse. Mounting behind her, Pavesi had the horse walk slowly back to the estate as Delvecchio raced ahead to order someone to get medical help.

The entire day and night was a battle to keep her alive. Early the following morning, the doctor had come down and notified them that her condition was getting no worse. She had passed the critical stage. Relieved, the household toasted to her health and waited for the arrival of Cangeliera. This Cangeliera character would know who had done this terrible act, thought Pavesi as he realized that he had begun slapping his gloves against his leg again.

Putting his fine leather gloves one atop the other on the table, he pondered what sort of beast would do such a thing. Unbelievable that Delvecchio had poisoned the bread. What had probably happened is that one of those rotten peasants had died from the bread and his mates sought revenge, thought Pavesi. Why did they pick Marina and not Delvecchio's stupid wife? Why my poor delicate flower? I dreamed of our wedding night when she would give herself to the first man — me.

Pavesi's impatience was getting the better of him, so he stood up and walked to the window hoping to see somebody; Cangeliera and Bellaria were some 20 feet from the door.

"Here they come!" exclaimed Pavesi.

Delvecchio stoop up anxiously.

"Good day to you," stated Santo Bellaria cheerfully as he and Cangeliera walked into the room. Hearing a distinctive click, they turned around to see Pavesi pointing his pistol at them.

"Listen," started Cangeliera.

"Shut up!" yelled Pavesi. "Shut up and listen to me!"

"Who did it? What pig did it?" questioned Delvecchio furiously.

"What are you talking about?" screamed the frightened Bellaria.

Faking perplexity, Cangeliera yelled; If what, are you people crazy? You ask me to come here and make a deal and then you ask us who did something that we don't know about? If this is some sort of game, let me tell you that I have twenty men out there who will wait and wait until the opportunity is right, and they then will kill you and your entire family. Put that gun down!" he ordered Pavesi.

"Put it down," said Delvecchio calmly. "I'm sorry, but a terrible thing has happened to my daughter. She was viciously attacked by one of your men. I will pay two hundred thousand lire for his head, he said coolly.

"Your daughter?" asked Bellaria. "She was raped? When?"

"Last night. Listen, enough of this. Do you know who did it?" asked Delvecchio.

"No," answered Cangeliera.

"Think, you bimbo. Think who could have done such a thing. Did anyone eat the bread?" asked Pavesi

"No, not really," stated Bellaria.

"What do you mean? Tell me everything that happened from the minute you left here last night. Maybe we can figure out who did it."

"Well','" said Bellaria, We rode for about an hour. Michael wanted to try some of the bread, but Salvatore tested it on a sheep. Salvatore is so smart, you know-"

"Continue with the story," snapped Pavesi.

"The sheep died. We threw the bread away and went to sleep. That's all, said Cangeliera knowing Bellaria would remember Michael's words.

"Did anyone say anything when the bread was discovered to be poisonous?" asked Pavesi.

"Well, just some joke, but Michael wouldn't do this," said Bellaria.

"What did he say?"

"Oh my God!" exclaimed Bellaria as he remembered Michael's words.

"What did he say?" repeated Pavesi impatiently.

"He said ... well, he said something about your daughter," mustered Bellaria in the direction of Delvecchio.

"What things" persisted Delvecchio?

"He said that he was going to ... going to ... you know," said Bellaria.

"That pig!" That disgusting pig!" screamed Delvecchio as he began to pace wildly around the room. Suddenly, he turned towards his wife's portrait and yanked it off the wall. Opening the safe, he pulled out two bulging sacks. Staring at Cangeliera and Bellaria, he walked over to the table and poured some two hundred thousand lire in notes onto the tabletop.

"I want his head!" he yelled. "I'll get you amnesty. I'll even get it in writing if you want, but I want his head."

Cangeliera couldn't help himself from glaring at the money, but Bellaria was shaking his head.

"Michael is my friend, I can't-"

"Do you want to see what he did to my daughter? Do you?" he asked hysterically. "Your band is going to acquire a very vile reputation if you don't clean out the garbage; this Michael is garbage. Even bandits don't rape wantonly. Then you are a pack of dogs."

"What does he look like?" questioned Pavesi.

"You know him," said Cangeliera to Delvecchio's puzzled look. He is the one that threatened your daughter in order to find out who killed Spilatieri. Remember?"

"What's this about a killing of Spilatieri?" asked Pavesi.

"One of our men was captured by the Gendarmes and executed by an officer by the name of Pavesi," replied Bellaria.

"He is Pavesi," stated Delvecchio as he watched the officer squirm in his tracks.

"Well, it was an accident. Really, anyway, that's history. Rather, let's discuss your freedom and your new found wealth," said Pavesi pointing to the hefty stacks of paper money on the table.

"We will accept your offer if the amnesty is written on an official document," said Bellaria sadly. "When you have the document, we will talk again. Agreed?"

Nodding in approval, Delvecchio gathered the money in the sacks and placed it back in the safe. Hesitating, he grabbed a handful of bills and walked over to the two outlaws. Placing money in their pockets, he wished them well and asked them to return in a week.

"Impossible. It must be sooner than that," said Cangeliera, realizing that the daughter, whom he had left for dead, would be in condition to recognize him.

"All right, then, come back in two days."

Cangeliera held up two fingers and smiled. Walking out the door, he hesitated, and then walked back into the house.

"By the way, Lieutenant," he said smiling, "you had better hide yourself, for Michael is after you. He will surely kill you if he finds you."

Looking over to Delvecchio, Cangeliera continued, "The quicker you get the paper, the better are his chances of living." Laughing, Cangeliera left the house.

"Well, where have you two been?" asked Salvatore as Cangeliera and Bellaria rode back into the camp.

"Oh just riding around. It's really a beautiful day today," responded Bellaria.

"Come over here, men," said Michael eagerly, "I think we should pay Delvecchio a visit. I think some big money is due to us for having attempted to poison us," laughed Michael.

The men laughed along, except for Cangeliera and Bellaria.

"I think it's a bad idea," snapped Cangeliera. "There are twenty Gendarmes over there. They are probably expecting us. It's a trap!" he exclaimed.

"If it were indeed a trap, they wouldn't be showing

all the Gendarmes," said Salvatore. "No, they are not expecting us at all."

'Veil, how are we to rid ourselves of the Gendarmes?"

"Easy, said Michael. We'll create a diversion."

"What kind of diversion?"

"A fire," answered Salvatore proudly. "A fire in their fields."

"Fantastic!" said Michael. "They will be too far away to hear or see anything. Pure genius, Salvatore!"

"Carlo, you and Mario will go start the fire. Make sure you get out of there quickly. Sandro, you steal their horses while the Gendarmes are fighting the fire. We will enter the house and be paid for the trick that Delvecchio tried to pull on us."

"All right, let's go."

Unwillingly, Cangeliera and Bellaria went with the group. Bellaria, highly concerned, was finally calmed by Cangeliera's assurances that Delvecchio would not give away their secret.

"Why should he?" said Cangeliera. "They want Michael dead. Delvecchio will not say anything."

"Sandro," yelled Salvatore, "Don't take the horses until we are out of sight. The Gendarmes will notice that the horses are missing, so you must give us enough time to get out of rifle range."

Mounting their horses, the group started for the Delvecchio estate. Carlo Bellaria and Mario Turisi went ahead to start the fire. Everyone was in good spirits for they imagined how stupid the Gendarmes would look when their horses had been stolen.

Book Characters

Charles Campo

Salvatore Campo

Salvatore's Younger Brother, Giuseppe

Salvatore

Grace

Frank and Rosalie

Michael and Angelina

Salvatore Campo

Salvatore and Giuseppe Campo

Giuseppe Campo, Salvatore's Brother

Giuseppe Campo

CHAPTER EIGHT

"SHE IS SLEEPING," answered Pavesi as he walked down the stairs from Marina's room.

"Thank God she is alive," said Delvecchio. "I don't know what I would have done if ...."

"Don't think about it." interjected Pavesi. "Want a drink?"

"Yes, but make it wine. God knows I need it." Pavesi poured two glasses of wine and walked over to where the baron was sitting.

"I wonder about those two, especially Cangeliera. I just don't trust him," said the lieutenant.

"What does it matter? I'm sure he'll do it. I'll give him the amnesty papers before he kills Moccia. When he comes for the money with proof of Moccia's death, you, my friend, will arrest him. We will show him a double-cross better than you see in the cinema! That peasant bastard has the nerve to bargain with me whose blood goes back to the rulers of the world! I'll cut him to ribbons, the simple gavone."

"What about the amnesty papers" asked Pavesi, confused?

"What about them? You will ask to see them and then you will burn them. As I said, what amnesty papers?" laughed Delvecchio.

Pavesi looked at the old man admiringly. The old bastard was pretty clever. Pretty damn clever, thought Pavesi.

"What about Marina?" Will you send her to Rome to fully recover? She must have a change of scenery to forget what happened to her here in her own house."

"Yes. I would appreciate it if you would accompany my daughter, if that's possible," said Delvecchio knowing well that it certainly was.

"I'll be honored and delighted to be her escort. You know, baron, for some time now, I've held your daughter in the highest ranks of my soul and I-"

"Cut the crap," laughed Delvecchio at the shocked Pavesi. I'm sorry, but I know you love her, Pavesi. Someday, I suppose, we should sit down together and talk of the future, but not now. Instead, why don't you pour some more wine? I need it badly."

"Certainly," answered Pavesi happily in that Delvecchio had finally seriously acknowledged his relationship with Marina.

"When will they appoint you captain of this province, Pavesi?"

"Soon, very soon, sir. My record and performance are free of stain."

"Don't you think that capturing this band would aid to hasten your promotion?" asked Delvecchio knowingly.

"Yes of course. In fact, I was hoping that the prisoner I had taken would give me some help, but the accident ...."

"Oh yes, he was shot while struggling for the guard's

118

pistol, wasn't he?"

"Yes, in the head."

"How convenient."

"What do you mean, sir?"

"Was the guard Sicilian?"

"I suppose so, but I fail to see any-"

Delvecchio was laughing loudly. Obviously, thought Pavesi, Delvecchio thought that the guard and Spilatieri had arranged the death, but who could do such a thing?

"I can't believe that you think that my captive asked to be shot. I mean-"

"Listen to me, you young fool," said Delvecchio. "The faster you learn what I am about to tell you, the faster you might become somebody and stay alive to boot. This is Sicily, not Milano. People have prides that are thicker than steel. Do you understand? Your victim knew he was going to die, so he aided the process, thereby eliminating any more pain. Forget everything you learned about human nature in the secondary school. Begin your new education today."

"But he must have hoped that-"

"There is no hope for them" laughed Delvecchio. "They know it. That's why they are so dangerous."

"I don't know-"

"You had better learn our ways, Oreste. That is, if you hope to survive here. You wouldn't be thinking of living elsewhere would you?"

"Well, I hadn't given it much thought, but-"

"Good, you should learn to love this island."

"FIRE!! Fire in the fields!" screamed a servant.

"Oh my God," roared Delvecchio.

"Let me handle it," said Pavesi.

"Fire. Just don't let it burn ray house down," sighed the exasperated Delvecchio.

Like a field marshal in battle, Pavesi ordered his sergeant to take control of the attachment of the men and go fight the field fire.

The proud lieutenant returned to the cool parlor and reassured Delvecchio that all was under control. Not caring one way or the other, the baron commanded that Pavesi pour some wine in their glasses. Pavesi responded like the consummate lackey he was destined to become. Delvecchio knew he had this inexperienced pup in his hip pocket.

"I'll take some also, lieutenant," said Michael Moccia as he, Salvatore, Cangeliera, and Bellaria burst into the parlor brandishing their rifles wildly and indiscriminately.

"Very good, Senior Moccia," laughed Delvecchio.

"How do you know my name, you pig?" questioned Michael loudly.

"Lieutenant Pavesi here knows everything."

Pavesi's heart stopped. Remembering what Cangeliera had told him, Pavesi stepped forward.

"Yes, my father, Colonel, told me that the strong leader of the band was named Moccia. He found out from a prisoner he captured several weeks ago" lied Pavesi.

"He's lying," said Salvatore, "You know as well as I do that Spilatieri would never talk."

"You killed Spilatieri, didn't you?" asked Michael as he walked towards the panic-stricken Pavesi.

"It was an accident!" trembled Pavesi.

"Haven't you done enough, you vilest of animals!" screamed Delvecchio. "My daughter is upstairs in shock, ruined for life because of your barbarous lust.

"What in the hell are you talking about, baron? What is wrong with your daughter?"

"Michael!" yelled Salvatore, "Michael, relax."

"She was brutally raped and left to die by him!" exclaimed the outraged Delvecchio as he pointed to Michael's shocked face.

"Wait, Michael!" ordered Salvatore. "Baron, what makes you think it was he?"

Clearly at the loss for words, Delvecchio tried to rack his brain. "Maybe because of the way he tried to find out who had killed Spilatieri."

"Remember what Michael said to the baron?" said Cangeliera softly as he cowered under Michael's stare.

"Listen, I'm innocent of these accusations," said Michael calmly. "I don't care if you don't believe me. Truly, I'm sorry about your daughter. Now," said Michael taking command of the situation. "Let's talk business baron. Put twenty thousand lire on the table or I'll shoot you down where you stand. We had a cordial agreement, and you were so kind to offer us your fresh bread. I should burn down your house for that. You are a crafty son, of a bitch, Delvecchio. You could teach us a few things about how to rob and steal."

Quickly, Delvecchio put the sum on the table. Putting the money into Salvatore's pocket Michael pointed at the baron.

"I'm a Sicilian man. I'm an honest man. I didn't touch your daughter, and you know it baron. I could be the poor girl's father, and as for you", thumping Pavesi on the chest, "you are a dead man. You will have a short career in this neck of the woods as protector of the rich and famous."

Quietly, they left the estate. For a few moments there was silence, and then someone began screaming about the horses.

"It's too bad," said Delvecchio.

"What is?" asked the still frightened Pavesi.

"I say it's too bad that Moccia must die. He is innocent."

"What makes you say that, sir?"

"I know, I just know. He's a real man. Too bad he must die."

"Why must he die then?" asked the confused Pavesi.

"Because, idiot, he's going to kill you. Do you need a gypsy fortune-teller to tell you what he has in store for your poor ass?"

Michael didn't say a word until they had reached the camp site. The men dismounted and continued laughing about the horseless Gendarmes. Salvatore and Michael, however, were not laughing.

"Something is going wrong," said Salvatore softly. "It's not what we intended, what we wanted. Who would do such a thing?"

"I have my suspicions."

"Yes. I know what you mean but it's only a hunch."

"Uh, huh," said Michael looking over at the laughing

Cangeliera, who was partaking in some gendarme joke.

"Why don't you come with me to Tramontane's?" said Salvatore. "I'm going to see Grazia there; she misses you terribly, you know."

"Yes," said Michael, "I'd love to talk to her, but Maria ... I don't know."

"Look, you must face it sometime, why not now and be over with it?"

"So much tragedy, so many people have died recently that I think the world is ending somehow."

"Please come with me," implored Salvatore.

"I suppose I should face Maria and, Grazia, well, I can talk to her about all of this. She may be able to help me. I know she will."

"Good. It is settled then, let's go right away. We can be there in a few hours' hard ride. Grazia arrives in the morning."

Collecting all the money for the men's families, Salvatore told them that Michael and he would be back in three days. Quickly packing their horses, Salvatore and Michael rode out of the camp towards Tramontane's farm.

Attempting to keep Michael from thinking about all his troubles, Salvatore talked about the German occupation of their town. Salvatore didn't know what prompted him to recall those memories. Michael and he lived well stealing from the Germans who were sensing that their days were numbered in Sicily. Michael had no place to store the gasoline he siphoned from military vehicles parked in front of the Marra Cafe. Salvatore unloaded gallons of turned wine to hard-drinking huns who understood nothing about dark wines. Salvatore convinced the skeptical enlisted men of Hitler's grand design that the taste was characteristic of that province.

Salvatore and Michael traded fresh figs, oranges, eggs and vegetables to the military men for clothing, generators, tools, and medicines. Huge stockpiles were stored within the town limits, heavily guarded with shoot-to-kill notices in glasses Italian posted everywhere. The soldiers and the local peasants both realized that the mountains of equipment, mistakenly warehoused in their town and not in North Africa, would fall into Yankee hands. Therefore, the Germans used the military brick-a-brack to buy them what few luxuries were obtainable in Caltasetta.

Michael and Salvatore had no qualms about stealing from the Germans. Not that they prayed for the Americans to trounce their Northern European neighbor. American bombs killed and wrecked as effectively as those made in Berlin, but Caltanissetta had dozens of its men living in New York, Boston, and Philadelphia who supported their families remaining in Villarosa every month with money earned in America. The American checks surpassed any of those sent from Canada, New Zealand, France or Australia. Salvatore reasoned that America must be the best land if its alien workers sent the most money. Michael enjoyed recounting those occupation days. The Germans were always demanding women. They ogled the young maidens.

Michael once led several young girls into a nearby

cave to escape a gang of rowdy drunken gestapo men who wanted their sexual appetites satisfied. The drunken German trio paraded to the house of Mrs. Meglio, who had three good looking daughters whom, tried as she might, she could not keep confined throughout the entire German occupation. This night, the Gestapo agents were determined to rape these Sicilian 'Vestal Virgins" no matter what. Salvatore remained hidden nearby Meglio's house to monitor their reactions when the lecherous trio found no young maidens to seduce. Mr. and Mrs. Meglio could offer no satisfactory explanation to the Gestapo agents. Salvatore intervened when one skinny, pimpled face agent grabbed Vincent Meglio by the throat to choke the whereabouts of his prized daughters from him.

Coolly Salvatore entered the tiny hovel.

"Gentlemen, why tire yourselves out and get nowhere with these people? I know places where you can find the thing you are after. It is several kilometers from Villarosa."

The place Salvatore had in mind belonged to a band of gypsies who tended to the sexual desires of the area men in need of sexual activities too sinful to allow one's wife to perform. The price of sexual favors was low in lire, but quite high in contracting virulent venereal disease. Only drunks and the sexual maniacs would lie down in the same straw with these diseased creatures that lived the hedonistic life.

Michael grinned openly, even chuckled a bit, as he recalled the scene.

Salvatore led them to the gypsy encampment and

instructed the reigning monarch of the gypsies as to what the three German officers wanted. The gypsy king, who hated Germans because of their policy of expulsion from every land they conquered, went along with Salvatore.

Salvatore then beat it back to the commander's office, next to the town post office. He demanded the thin, bespectacled clerk to allow him to see Major Strimel. Major Strimel was too Catholic, even for the devout, Sicilian wives. He ran his army post the way a Monsignor would run an orphaned boys' home.

The Sicilians couldn't believe that being a Catholic was such hard work. Even Father Muccio tried to tone-down the over-zealous follower of Christ. Salvatore felt sure that Major Strimel would not reveal him to the three Gestapo men risking acquiring the ancient illness. In fact, Major Strimel would thank Salvatore for saving three members of his military flock. He quickly related to the bald, shiny-headed commandant that he has just returned from the gypsy encampment and saw the three Gestapo agents negotiating the terms of their sexual requirements. He gave Strimel the most direct route to the den of iniquity. Strimel phoned Seidel, the chief of all Gestapo and also a daily communicant along with Strimel at seven a.m. mass, and asked that he accompany him to save these depraved souls. Salvatore begged Strimel to preserve his anonymity or he would be killed.

"Signor Campo, because we are at war doesn't mean that we have no morals. I respect you for placing yourself in jeopardy to save another Christian soul as yourself. You have my guarantee that no one will ever know who cared enough to stop them. I only hope we are in time to save the poor fools."

Salvatore rounded-up Michael at the grotto where he was protecting the Meglio girls. He and Michael raced to the encampment on a motorcycle Salvatore had borrowed from the town mayor.

Salvatore and Michael arrived just before the huge Mercedes reached the campfire grounds. They worked as Enzo, the chief gypsy, greeted the austere party, realizing that sex was not their bidding, but retribution. He pointed to a tent -where Seidel's three aides were doing sexual gymnastics with a bevy of gypsy paramours. They gypsy women fled, raising the tent skirts and scurrying into the thicket naked. Michael and Salvatore giggling boyishly heard the tirade. The three German sinners couldn't put their civilian clothing on fast enough, as Seidel prognosticated their military career — the Russian front.

The gypsies raced frantically to break camp and escape the Russian wrath. The Mercedes staff car remained unattended and Michael slit the thickly treaded dirt tires with his black stiletto. Michael had no idea who in the German military hierarchy could be informed next of the whereabouts of the famed Africa corps. Enough was enough—the Meglio girls remained pure for some provincial boy to have, the three German maladroit were relocated to endure their justified disease in colder climates, and Strimel and Seidel were certain that their good work would win them eternal salvation in heaven.

"You know, Salvatore, life was simple when the

Germans were here. We used our energy and cleverness to outwit them and enjoyed it. We played games. Now we play for keeps."

His heart pounding, Michael followed Salvatore through the entrance of Tramontane's house. Maria was walking into the room with a large plate of polenta in her hands which she immediately dropped. Wanting to rush up to Michael, she let only her eyes to so, for her husband was sitting at the table.

"Let me help you," said Salvatore as he bent over to pick up the remnants of the plate.

"I'll go get some rags," she muttered as she burst out of the room.

"Michael, how are you?" asked Tramontane.

"Fine," he lied.

"I'm sorry about Rosalia," he said as his voice dropped off.

"I mean to thank you for all you did. I don't know how I can ever repay you for your kindness," said Michael thinking of how guilty he felt about his affair with Maria.

'Veil, I'm glad Maria was here to help you through those first few hours. She told tie you took it real bad at first."

"Yes, she was very kind. I must thank her."

"Come, come. Both of you come and eat. Salvatore, get off the ground!" said Tramontane.

Both of the men walked over to the table and sat down. Michael was praying that Maria wouldn't come.

"So Grazia arrives in the morning, huh?" asked Tramontano of Salvatore.

"Yes, I can't wait to see her and the children. It seems like years since I've seen them."

"I bet. What do you boys plan to do?"

"Oh, I think we will go see the Mafioso Lipiani. He is powerful and wise; he may give us some advice and hopefully, some protection."

"Not a bad idea," confirmed Tramontane as Maria walked in the room with yet another plate of polenta.

"Are you two hungry?" she asked kindly.

"Famished," laughed Salvatore.

"Yes," said Michael unconvincingly.

"I must hurry because I have to go into town on some business. I'll be back late tonight, though," said Tramontano.

Maria's and Michael's eyes met as Salvatore squirmed in his chair.

After they had eaten, the three men continued to drink some wine. Soon, Tramontano stood up and declared that he was off on some business.

"Maria," he called. "Maria."

"Yes," she answered from the kitchen.

"I'm leaving now. Don't wait for me to eat tonight. Take good care of our guests."

Salvatore watched Tramontano's carriage disappear in the distance.

"Well I'm going out hunting for some rabbits for tomorrow. I'll be back in a couple of hours."

"No, don't," whispered Michael.

"Go and talk to her, Michael. I'm leaving for at least two hours," said Salvatore as he walked out the door.

Michael sat in the parlor in silence for at least half an hour. When Maria walked in the room, he was staring out the window. Startling him, she sat next to him.

"How are you Michael?" she asked gently.

"Not so well. I thought often of you in these days. In fact, I don't seem able to stop thinking of you."

"I know what you mean. What shall we do?"

Maria's question startled Michael. He had never confronted the problem as being solvable. Always assuming that there was nothing they could do, Michael had resigned himself to thinking of beautiful memories of a desperate night. Her tone and, obviously, her question drew his attention to the fact that indeed there were several possibilities. Whether they were feasible was an entirely different matter; nevertheless, he acknowledged for the first time - perhaps, for the first time in his life - that a situation would be altered.

"I know what I would like to do," he answered sadly, as if indicating that this desire could never be fulfilled.

"Yes, but what are you going to do about it?" she asked forcefully.

"I don't know, Maria," he continued, "I'm very confused about many things. Having suffered greatly, I am not very clear with my thoughts, my plans. My life has changed so radically in the last few months. First Franco, now Rosalia and my poor children, dead. All of them are dead. Everything around me is sick and dying except you. You are my only life, the only warmth that I feel."

"Shall we run away together?"

"Where?"

"Anywhere."

"What about your husband?"

"He can live without me, you can't."

"So you pity me, is that it?"

"Don't be stupid. It's got nothing to do with pity. I love you. I love you for the way you love me."

"Oh, so it's sexual," he teased.

"Yes, speaking of which, I want to show you something in my room."

"Sure, I bet it's interesting," laughed Michael.

"Come with me, little boy," she said standing up.

Salvatore was up before dawn. Anxiously awaiting Grazia's arrival, he lit a cigarette and immediately put it out. He dressed quickly and he silently walked out of the room so as not to wake Michael. Would Grazia think that her brother had gone mad? No, Salvatore doubted it. There was nobody who understood Michael better than she did. Certainly, she could help Michael's tormented mind.

Salvatore laughed as he thought about the previous afternoon. When he had walked into the parlor he had heard them gasping and panting in her bedroom. He must be something else for her to take such wild chances. Of course, he was special; he was, after all, Salvatore's best friend. Salvatore had known him for over twenty years. Twenty years'.

Michael has always suffered greatly. Now, in these unfortunate times, it seemed that he was again carrying the burden of pain. Horror after horror came to visit Michael, thought Salvatore. It was uncanny how everything seemed to happen to him.

Walking towards the gates, Salvatore pondered over his brother-in-law's misfortunes when his heart leaped for joy. Grazia and his children had just become visible to him. Running like a maniac, be began screaming out his wife's name.

When he finally embraced her and his children, Salvatore began to cry not only out of joy, but also out of loneliness, the loneliness he had bottled up inside of himself for weeks. For a few days, at least, Salvatore would be at peace with the world.

CHAPTER **NINE**

THE NEWS FROM Villarosa was not good. Unemployment affected everyone. Hunger was fast becoming a harsh reality. The people grew desperate.

Many groups had organized throughout Sicily in an attempt to combat starvation. The number of robberies and related crimes soared. To Salvatore's dismay, many of these crimes were being blamed on his gang.

The Mafioso Cateno Riotta, Santo and Carmine's uncle, had recounted several distressing tales to Grazia. Apparently, some landowners had bought gangs and arranged for the slaughter or rival groups. In this manner, the landowners obviously hoped that the gangs would eliminate each other. Imploring Salvatore to use extreme caution, Grazia told him of an encounter she had had with the Mafioso Lipiani.

Giorgio Lipiani was, in the tradition of the Mafiosi, a wise and powerful man. His counsel, as well as his protection, was sought by many in the area. In fact, Salvatore's group had planned to visit him, and Salvatore was therefore pleased to hear of Lipiani's visit to his home.

"Why did he come to see you?" asked Salvatore.

"He had heard of our troubles. He wants to talk to your gang. There are terrible things going on. I think you should meet with him," said Grazia with a concerned look on her face.

"Where shall we meet him? I mean-"

"He has asked to see Michael and Santo Bellaria at our house. They are to meet him there in six days, in the early part of the morning."

"Wait a minute! Why Michael and Santo?"

"Lipiani said that he wants to talk to them and them only. He specifically requested that neither you nor Cangeliera be there ... for safety," said Grazia knowing how preoccupied Salvatore would be during the meeting if he were absent. "You see, you and Cangeliera are wanted ... there is a reward," she said sighing. "Please don't worry, though, everything will be all right." Her eyes radiated uncertainty.

Nodding, Salvatore peered into Grazia's eyes. It seemed like ages since he had seen her eyes. Grazia, thought Salvatore, had the most expressive eyes he had ever seen.

When they had first started seeing each other, Salvatore would always look into Grazia's eyes. She had large, brown, sad eyes that seemed to directly reflect her soul. Most often, Salvatore remembered, her eyes would display that unique combination of boredom, sadness and emptiness; however, on those rare occasions when she would laugh from happiness, her eyes would project a mystical, teasing joy that swept everyone into a pleasant state of mind. Often, Salvatore would be amazed at what a transformation she could make from one mood to another.

Actually, it wasn't until Grazia was around fourteen

that Salvatore began to notice her. Before that time, she was merely Michael's little sister, who adored her brother, and therefore, wanted to be with them. So many times the boys refused her futile attempts to accompany them. Michael, Salvatore and Franco certainly did not want a girl with them! Not then.

On the night of Grazia's fourteenth birthday, the three inseparable friends decided to attend her simple party. Having had other plans, the boys made this decision due to Michael's father's threats to make life hard for him if he did not attend his sister's party.

Michael was devouring the party food and Salvatore and Franco were standing around perfectly bored by the whole affair when Grazia walked into the room. Deeply tanned, her new white dress contrasted sensuously with her laughing, teasing eyes. Long, brownish, wavy hair fell over her shoulders halfway down her back. Smiling triumphantly, she walked across the room happily returning Salvatore's stare. Gesturing towards the food, she suggested to the still awestruck Salvatore that he should try some of the food.

"It's pretty good," mumbled Michael who was seated at the table eating.

Walking over towards Grazia, Salvatore, accompanied by a giggling Franco, accepted the offer.

"You look ... uh ... very good," snapped Salvatore nervously.

"Thank you," she smiled.

"So you are fourteen today, huh? You are really growing up fast," said Salvatore as Franco elbowed him in the back. Turning around to face Franco, Salvatore was greeted by his friend's rolling eyes that sharply reminded him not to stare at Grazia's breasts when making comments on her growth rate.

"Ah," exclaimed Michael as he rose from the table having noticed Salvatore's reaction to his sister. "Isn't she beautiful? She will be the most beautiful woman in Villarosa. Don't you agree, Salvatore?"

"Yes," stammered Salvatore.

Ever since that day, the little girl whose pleas had so often been denied was suddenly allowed to accompany the trio. Salvatore's growing interest in Grazia pleased Michael and Grazia, but it was hardly well received by her parents. Nevertheless, Michael's influence along with Grazia's desires overcame that formidable obstacle.

Grazia quickly became the fourth friend of the group. Her gender had hampered the four-way relationship at first, but her persistence led her to total acceptance. After several months, she was a full member of the trinity.

Salvatore and Grazia's relationship was not much different than her friendship with her brother or with Franco. In a sense, she treated Salvatore as the preferred brother; she would often be in some sort of physical contact with him, whether it was a kidding punch on the shoulder or a request for being held due to the cold weather or fatigue or fright. Their closeness was innocuous enough at first, but Michael did finally begin to think that she was beginning to be a little old for the roughhouse antics that she was enjoying with Salvatore.

"What do you think of my sister?" questioned Michael

one day in her absence.

"What do you mean? She is a nice kid." answered Salvatore puzzled.

"I mean, what do you really think of her? Do you-"

"Get to the point," laughed Salvatore.

'Veil, do ... do you like her?"

"Yes," he smiled at Michael's uneasiness.

"I mean do you really like her? You know!" said Michael seriously.

"I know she's young, but ... well, yes! I do."

"Let me get this straight. Do you love her as a woman or-"

"Well, I've never thought of it that way."

"Think about it," said Michael softly. "I mean this brotherly thing is a little strange, don't you think?"

Several days later in a rare moment that found Salvatore and Grazia alone, he approached her with a rather serious expression on his face.

"Grazia, I ... I must speak with you."

"What is it?" she asked.

"I ... well I wanted to ... I think ... let me see. All right, I like you very much. "

"I like you too." she said innocuously.

"No, no. You don't understand-"

"Oh yes I do," she said emphatically as she put her arms around him and kissed him. Giggling, she ran into the house.

The extent of their relationship was never clearly defined, in that it would waiver between passion and friendly affection. Long conversations and several years aided the mutual attachment in becoming progressively solidified, but it wasn't until the Franco Di Meglio carriage situation that Salvatore felt obliged to take a serious stand.

At first, Michael and Salvatore used to laugh about the merchant from Palermo, but gradually Salvatore became jealous. Though hardly enamored with Di Meglio, Grazia was amused by his gifts, attitude, and especially, his attention to her every whim, need or desire. Noticing Salvatore's increasing jealousy, she was flattered at first - until it became clear that the situation may backfire on her. Actually, Grazia Moccia was somewhat relieved when the Di Meglio situation was abruptly terminated by a wild Michael.

Immediately after the departure of Di Meglio, the relationship between Grazia and Salvatore changed radically. They became officially in love and acted accordingly. Salvatore recalled the incessant desire in his soul to be with her. Grazia and Salvatore became inseparable and, with much crying, she was able to obtain her parents' blessing. They were married on a fair day in April. Grazia was nineteen, Salvatore, twenty-five.

Then her eyes were happy and care-free. That was the past.

Salvatore sighed as he looked away from Grazia's eyes.

"How's Michael?" she asked, preoccupied.

"Not well. He needs to talk to you. Go to him."

Opening the barn door slowly, Grazia saw her sleeping brother crouched on some hay. Asleep, he appeared to be care-free, even happy. Grazia knew better, though. Michael was fated to be miserable.

"Michael," she whispered as she sat down next to her brother. Kissing him on the cheek she reiterated her call. "Michael, wake up. It's me, Grazia."

"Oh Grazia. How are you?" he asked still half asleep.

'Veil, a fine brother you are!" she said feigning anger. "I come all this way to see you and-"

"Grazia!" yelled Michael finally realizing what was taking place. Pulling her towards him, he gave her a loud emphatic kiss on the cheek, to which she responded by rubbing a handful of hay in his face. Laughing, she jumped up.

"I'm so glad to see you," said Michael eagerly. "There is so much that I want to tell you-"

"I'll bet," she said in a mock serious tone.

"What do you mean?"

"How are farmers wives these days, big brother?" she teased.

"Oh Grazia I feel so terrible about ..."

Realizing that her tone was not in line with his feelings on the matter, she quickly attempted to put him at ease.

"It's all right. Actually, I'm rather proud of you. She is rather a fancy lady, isn't she?"

Michael smiled sheepishly. "I feel so guilty towards Rosalia that I-"

"No, no no! You needed her and she would have seen it your way. Life must go on. You know, I used to feel the same way when I made love to Salvatore before we were married-"

"YOU WHAT!" yelled Michael faking anger so well that Grazia actually began to fear the consequences of her statement.

"Hey, listen that was the past and besides look at you."

"Where is he? I'm going to kill that dirty bastard!" yelled Michael, thoroughly enjoying the joke he was pulling on Grazia.

Knowing her brother as well as she did, Grazia soon realized that he was faking; therefore, she decided she would really shake him up with a few lies that would completely reverse the joker-joked upon relationship.

"Actually," she continued trying her best to appear serious. "I felt most guilty about Franco, but then again the way Giacomo made love to me and Di Meglio ... Antonio, Giuseppe ..."

By this time she had run out of the barn laughing hysterically while Michael attempted to chase her.

"All right, you win!" screamed Michael half-laughing.

"Damn right I do!"

The following days were spent in long conversations, hearty laughter and general good cheer. Endless hours were spent with Grazia, Maria, and Salvatore in discussion with Michael. The warmth he felt from his sister, his lover and his best friend was enough to keep Michael going. The depths of depression were slowly beginning to fade as his friends seemed to rejuvenate his spirit.

Though nothing was actually resolved, the pure energy he felt from them seemed to be transplanted in his soul. Their caring and affection gave him new strength,

strength to face the onslaught of new misfortunes that might be coming his way.

Dawn came to an awaken household the morning of the day that Michael and Salvatore were to leave. Having agreed to bring the band to Villarosa so that Michael and Bellaria could meet Lipiani, Salvatore unwillingly mounted his horse. Michael kissed Maria, then Grazia.

Tears came to Grazia as she waved her husband and her brother goo-bye. Grazia would never see Michael again.

CHAPTER **TEN**

IT WAS LATE in the afternoon when Michael and Salvatore rode into their camp. The sharp January winds howled about their ears, thereby promising an unusually cold winter. Anxiously, Bellaria and Cangeliera greeted the two men as they dismounted and headed towards the fire. Letting the fiery warmth expel all the remnants of cold from their stiff bodies, Michael and Salvatore recounted various events about Villarosa that Grazia had relayed to them at Tramontane's farm.

Annoyed, even angry, Cangeliera reacted violently to the news that the gang was being blamed for crimes they did not commit. Encouraged by the fact that the Mafioso Lipiani was to meet them and possibly help them, the group decided that they would head for Villarosa in the morning.

"What else did my uncle tell Grazia?" asked Bellaria of Salvatore as Michael handed Salvatore a plateful of warm food.

"Not much. Oh yes, he did say that some landowners were putting rival gangs against each other. He warned that we should use extreme caution in dealing with other gangs."

"Can you believe it?" yelled Cangeliera. "All of us are in the same horrible situation, yet we kill each other instead of the rich."

"They aren't rich because they are stupid," noted Bellaria.

"By the way," Cangeliera asked Salvatore, "Why does he want to meet Moccia and Santo? Why not us?"

"We are wanted. I guess he feels that it is safer for them."

"I suppose someone would turn us in for the reward," said Cangeliera dismayed. "In these days, such a thing would be possible, even likely."

"I'm afraid so."

Light snow, relatively rare for Sicily, woke the gang up the next morning. Slowly gathering their belongings, the men packed their horses in preparation for the trip back to Villarosa. After nearly half an hour of chatting, the men finally moved out of the carp into the frosty wind. The group had enough provisions to last nearly a month, so they could afford to make the trip without stopping for food. Bypassing the Tramontane farm, the group headed for Villarosa's San Giacomo chapel.

The chapel was an ideal place for the gang to wait as Michael and Bellaria went to see Lipiani. Wearing black hooded cloaks, Michael and Bellaria walked their horses slowly through the streets of Villarosa. Luckily, the cold was keeping most of the city dwellers in their homes, thus permitting their journey to Salvatore's home to be uneventful.

After walking several miles, the two men finally approached Salvatore's house. Nervously pacing the kitchen floor, Giorgio Lipiani greeted the cold, drenched men.

"Don Lipiani, how good it is to see you," stated Bellaria formally.

"Giorgio! How are you?" was Michael's eager greeting to the anxious Lipiani.

"Fine, fine." Looking at Michael, Lipiani continued, "Grazia is at Angelina's house. I didn't want..."

"We understand," interrupted Michael smiling.

"Well, sit down and let's get down to business, shall we?" motioned Lipiani as he pulled out chair and presently sat down. Following suit, Michael began asking Lipiani what the gang should do.

"There are many complications," said Lipiani coldly. "The barons have united. Their money is buying them protection from various gangs who, at the request of their bosses, are killing off smaller gangs. You must be careful. I suggest you always move quickly and backtrack often. Maybe you should leave the area for a while."

"But why are the people doing this?" questioned Michael furiously. "Why don't they just steal from the barons themselves?"

"The war is almost over. Many Gendarmes will return and fight for the barons and other landlords. Your gang should offer some powerful baron protection if you hope to obtain amnesty after the war. You can't win, you know. They will eventually crush you if you don't play along with them."

"What do you suggest we do, then?" asked Bellaria, whose obvious preoccupation with the situation at hand was making Lipiani nervous.

"The way I see it, you have two choices. First of all,

you must realize that you have been accused of several murders as well as the rape of the Delvecchio girl. Anyway, what I am trying to say is that if you are caught, you are finished. There is a brash young Lieutenant, a Paveso, Pavese, I forget his name-"

"Pavesi," interjected Michael, momentarily recalling Giuseppe Spilatieri.

"Yes, Pavesi," continued Lipiani wondering how Michael was so well informed. "As I was saying, this Pavesi character has promised to hang all of you as a wedding present to his future father-in-law-"

"You mean he and the Delvecchio daughter?" asked Bellaria.

"Exactly. Obviously, he thinks your gang is responsible for the rape," Lipiani said looking at Michael.

"He thinks I did it but I swear-"

"Never mind," snapped Lipiani. "The point is that you all need protection. Either you get protection from a baron or you all leave the country. Maybe for America."

Lipiani's words weighed heavily on Michael's soul. Neither choice was appealing, but he felt that he would do almost anything to stay in Sicily. What would he do in America? Shuddering at the thought, Michael glared over at Bellaria, who was deep in thought.

Lipiani stood up and walked over to the comer. Picking up a wine flask, he poured three glasses full of red wine and then sat down again. Looking at the depressed faces opposite him, Lipiani cleared his throat in an attempt to recall the men from the depths of their thoughts.

"Michael, do you remember Baron Francesco Riccardi? You and Salvatore worked for him one summer. All right, then, I have spoken to him about the need for a strong gang to protect his properties. I mentioned to him about your situation and he has agreed to talk to you. Tomorrow, I'll go see him and try to arrange a meeting. He's a powerful man and can surely manage to offer you amnesty. What do you think?"

Michael nodded enthusiastically but was annoyed by Bellaria's lack of attention.

"What do you think, Bellaria?" asked Michael angrily.

"Oh, I'm sorry ... Yes, yes of course. It would be fantastic, I think."

"Great!" interrupted Michael annoyed. "How will you let us know when we are to meet him?"

"I'll go and see him then I'll meet all of you at Tramontane's. Agreed?"

Bellaria was again immersed in his thoughts. Michael was to blame for all our problems, he mused. Looking at Michael, Bellaria began to hate him intensely. Why did he have to rape that girl? He was indeed a pig. The Baron Delvecchio had offered him and Cangeliera amnesty if they would kill Michael. At first Bellaria had been reluctant, but by now in face of all these distressing facts, he realized that he had no choice. Delvecchio was the most powerful baron in the area, he could get them amnesty. Anyway, why should he have to pay for the disgusting acts committed by Michael? To hell with Lipiani and his 'possibilities', thought Bellaria. Cangeliera and he had amnesty from Delvecchio as soon as they finished with

146

Michael. Thinking of a way that he and Cangeliera could separate Michael from, the group without arousing suspicion, Bellaria's thoughts were suddenly interrupted by a sharp push on the arm.

"What are you doing?" yelled Michael, visibly angry. "This may be the most important advice we get and you daydream like an idiot!"

Lipiani laughed; Bellaria mused on the pleasure he would have in killing Michael. We shall see who the real idiot is, he thought angrily.

"I'm sorry," Bellaria muttered.

"Forget it. Listen Giorgio, when will you meet us then?" asked Michael.

"The day after tomorrow at Tramontano's farm."

Agreeing, Michael stood up indicating that it was time for them to leave. Asking Lipiani to give his sister a hug from him, Michael nodded to Bellaria. Putting their monks' tunics on in silence, the two men hid their shotguns under their outer garments and headed for the door.

"Good luck," said Lipiani.

"Thanks. We will need it, I'm sure," replied Michael.

"Let's go," said Bellaria, shuddering at the cold winter wind that sliced through their clothes as he opened the door. Grabbing their horses' reins, the men slowly walked through the cold deserted streets of Villarosa.

"Can you believe this weather?" asked Bellaria as they approached the pasta factory on the way to the chapel.

"I don't remember a winter like this one," remarked Michael. Suddenly it started to snow lightly. "Actually,

I've only seen snow two other tines in my life."

"You know," said Bellaria, "the first time that I saw snow, I got so scared that I wouldn't go out of the house. I was about six years old. The morning that I woke up and saw all the whiteness all over the ground, I thought the world had ended." Bellaria laughed.

"Michael Moccia, don't move!" barked a voice from the direction of the pasta factory. Slowly Michael turned around to see five Gendarmes pointing their guns at them.

"Oh, no'." gasped Bellaria.

Michael wished that Salvatore were there, but in his absence, Michael knew that he would have to think of something quickly.

"What do you want of me?" Michael directed his question in the direction of a sergeant, obviously the man in charge.

"You," the sergeant laughed. He ordered, "Step away from your horses and put your hands up."

"Use the horse as your protection," whispered Michael to Bellaria as he planned his move.

Trembling, Bellaria watched Michael and was ready to move when he did. Suddenly, Michael whirled to the horse's side, thereby shielding his body with the horse's flanks. Following suit, Bellaria began to run along with Michael down the snowy road.

Gunfire crackled through the cold air. Racing away from the Gendarmes, Michael saw Bellaria's horse fall to the ground, hit by the Gendarmes. Trying to hold his own panic-stricken horse, Michael ordered Bellaria to flatten himself against the ground. Suddenly Michael's horse lunged ahead and ran rapidly away from him. Diving for cover, Michael was hit in the right arm. Whirling completely around, Michael screamed loudly as he crawled for cover. Bellaria, rushing to aid Michael, was hit in the wrist.

Swearing under his breath, Michael stood himself up by pushing his back against the wall and using his legs to elevate his torso. Pulling out his shotgun, he shot in the direction of the Gendarmes in order to slow down their advance.

"Pull out your gun!" gasped Michael to a moaning Bellaria.

"I can't, I-"

"Do it with your other hand! Just pull it out and start shooting. Hopefully the others will hear and come to get us out of this mess," said Michael as he propped his shotgun on his right forearm and quickly stepped out into the street. Diving immediately for cover, he whistled aloud as four shots whizzed by his previous position.

"When I say go, start running for a few seconds down the street. I'll cover you, then you do the same for me. We must keep it constantly going so as to stop them from advancing. I'm going to the other side of the street. Cover me. Ready?"

Michael ran across the street followed closely by several gunshots. Arriving safely to the other side, he nodded for Bellaria, then stepped out into the street and began shooting while Bellaria ran for some sixty yards. Bellaria then stopped and began opening fire on the Gendarmes, which permitted Michael to run. In this manner, Michael and Bellaria were able to gradually move toward the chapel.

About ten minutes later, the en heard more gunshots as they saw Cangeliera, Salvatore and the others racing down the street. Stopping as they noticed Michael and Bellaria, the group dismounted and kept covering the men.

"Let's go after them," said Cangeliera pointing in the direction of the five fleeing Gendarmes.

"We have to get these two to a doctor," responded Salvatore, annoyed at Cangeliera's idiotic suggestion.

Looking at Michael and Bellaria, Cangeliera seemed to recall their existence and agreed with Salvatore's suggestion.

Bleeding profusely, the weakening Michael was hoisted onto Salvatore's horse as Bellaria rode with Cangeliera. Turning around, the gang raced out of Villarosa.

Realizing that their presence in the area was dangerous, the gang decided to head for Tramontane's, where they felt the men would get adequate medical attention for Maria. Suggesting that a doctor would be in order, Cangeliera volunteered to go to Delvecchio's estate where there was a doctor that was taking care of Marina. In this manner, thought Cangeliera, I'll have a chance to talk to Delvecchio about amnesty without arising suspicion.

Departing from the group at the outskirts of Villarosa, Cangeliera rode through the night. As the sun was beginning its long journey through the sky, the Delvecchio estate became visible to Cangeliera.

Riding right up to the front door, Cangeliera handed the reins to a servant and walked into the parlor. Being informed that the household was still asleep. Cangeliera decided to wait for Delvecchio before requesting a doctor. Accepting an offer to eat, Cangeliera sat down at the kitchen table and listened impatiently to the cook's story of his experience with snow.

'Veil, well, how are you Mister Cangeliera?" asked Baron Delvecchio as Cangeliera jumped up apologetically.

"I have come for a doctor, some men are hurt, I came for the amnesty papers."

"Not so fast, Cangeliera. What insures me that you will indeed kill Moccia?" asked Delvecchio, knowing exactly what Cangeliera's response would be.

"We will do it, Baron," laughed Cangeliera, "Because we want the money. Remember, the money?"

"How could I forget?" teased the baron as he motioned for Cangeliera to follow him. Once in the parlor, Delvecchio headed for the safe where he pulled out two large documents.

Handing the paper to Cangeliera, he watched Cangeliera laboriously read the contents of the documents. Smiling at the thought of Cangeliera's expression when he would realize that he was about to be arrested, Delvecchio couldn't wait for Cangeliera's return from his murderous deed.

"I hope you are duly satisfied," said the baron calmly. "Oh yes, this is terrific," responded Cangeliera with an enthusiasm that was impossible for him to hide. "We will be back soon."

"When do you expect soon to be?" questioned Delvecchio.

"I suspect that Moccia will be dead very soon," smiled Cangeliera at the receptive baron.

"The sooner, the better. My friend the lieutenant is very impatient to clear up this matter. You see, he is to marry my daughter and wants all memories of the horrible act permanently removed from this earth. You can understand his impatience, can't you", asked Delvecchio, hoping that Cangeliera would quickly fulfill his promise; Delvecchio feared for Pavesi's life.

Agreeing, Cangeliera inquired about the doctor, to which Delvecchio lied by stating that he had left due to his daughter's speedy recovery. Upset, Cangeliera was calmed by Delvecchio's statement indicating the presence of another doctor in the vicinity.

"By the way, where is Lieutenant Pavesi?" inquired Cangeliera nervously.

"He has gone to Rome with my daughter," lied Delvecchio.

"When will they be married, then?"

"In about two months. Why do you ask?"

"Oh, I just wanted to send them a present, nothing important, just a thought, you know. Well, I suppose I should be off. I must go visit the doctor," smiled Cangeliera.

"See you soon, then?"

"Yes, yes," responded Cangeliera nervously as he walked out the door.

Watching Cangeliera ride off in the distance, Delvecchio pondered over how much he distrusted this bandit. Turning slowly around, the smiling Delvecchio walked toward his favorite wine. As he held up the wine in order to appreciate its color, he saw his daughter Marina standing at the top of the stairway.

White as a ghost, she stood there speechless, trembling uncontrollable, staring at the door as if she had just seen the devil himself.

"Marina!" yelled the shocked Delvecchio, as the awful realization crept up his spine. Whirling about to see if he could spot the far gone Cangeliera, he swore under his breath.

Completely enraged, he smashed the wine bottle on the floor.

"Pavesi. PAVESI!! he screamed. "Get Pavesi up!" he yelled at his servant. "PAVESI!"

CHAPTER **ELEVEN**

MARIA TRAMONTANE BURST out of her house as she saw Michael on Salvatore's horse.

"What happened?" she cried.

"There was some shooting, Michael and Santo Bellaria got hurt."

"Put them in my room," she ordered as she raced back into the house. Once in the kitchen, Maria frantically threw some water in a large pot and raced to the linen closet to get some clean towels.

Running to her room, she supervised the placing of Michael and Bellaria on her bed. Ordering the men to strip them of their wet, cold clothes, she asked a servant to get some clothes from her husband's closet. Asking Salvatore to undress the two injured men, Maria walked quickly out of the room towards the kitchen.

Waiting for the water to boil, Maria scooped the knives out of the pot onto the towels. Ordering the servant to follow her with the pan of water, Maria ran out of the kitchen after having sterilized the knives again over the open fire.

Entering the bedroom, she saw Salvatore trying to put a shirt on Michael.

"No. Stop. Don't put the shirt on," she snapped. "Where was he hit?" she asked as she saw the shattered tissue on Michael's arm.

Turning his head towards her, the silent Michael seemed to beg her to action. Snapping out of a daze, she moved quickly to his side. Offering him a towel to bite on, she was about to begin, but his eyes refused the towel as he remained perfectly still, looking intensely at Maria.

Nervously, she held his arm and inspected the wound.

"In the meantime, look after Bellaria," she ordered her servant as she found the bullet buried deep into Michael's bicep. Asking Salvatore to hold Michael's arm, she used a thin strong knife to pry the bullet out of his muscle. To everyone's surprise, Michael didn't flinch; Bellaria was screaming hysterically.

Salvatore watched his friend staring at Maria. His hypnotic stare was somewhat distracting to her, but she felt tremendous courage in his trust in her. Quickly and thoroughly cleaning the wound, she dressed it and finally asked the men to help her put his shirt on. Silently, Michael kept staring at Maria.

"Are you comfortable?" she asked kindly.

Michael didn't answer, but his eyes began to fill up with tears. Confused, she repeated her question. Michael turned his head away from her.

"Maybe we should let him sleep," whispered Salvatore to a perplexed Maria.

"Yes," she answered. "He must be in a state of shock. Yes, that's it, shock." She walked slowly out of her bedroom followed by Salvatore and the others.

Deciding that Bellaria should be moved, since he

would probably keep Michael awake all the night, Salvatore and Carlo Bellaria reentered the room to move Bellaria. As Salvatore was leaving her room, Michael called him back.

"Tell her that I love her," Salvatore nodded.

"You, Maria and Grazia are all I have. I love you all so much," sighed Michael.

"Try to get some sleep," said Salvatore softly.

"All right."

Closing the door behind him, Salvatore wondered what had triggered Michael's strange mood. Walking into the kitchen, he saw Maria staring out the window.

"He told me to tell you that he loves you."

Smiling, she hugged Salvatore and went in the direction of her room. Salvatore smiled inwardly as he realized how cleverly she had engineered the situation so that she could be along with Michael.

It was early evening when Cangeliera arrived with the doctor. Insisting that he see his patients immediately, Salvatore guided the doctor to Bellaria, then he went to see Michael to tell him that the doctor was about to pay a visit. Knocking loudly on the door, he heard Maria give a light scream as she obviously scampered to dress herself. After several long moments, she opened the door trying her best at nonchalance.

"Excuse me for asking, but amidst all this confusion I have forgotten to ask you where your husband was," said Salvatore.

"Rome, looking for more property that I suggested he invest in," she smiled.

"You are too much. By the way, the doctor is here and wants to see Michael. I thought I'd warn you so as to prevent a scandal," whispered Salvatore laughingly.

"Sometimes I wonder whether you enjoy this more than I do," she said with benign sarcasm as she slipped by him and headed into the kitchen.

Several weeks passed by. The men were becoming restless. Maria was dismayed due to her husband's immanent arrival and Lipiani never showed up. Convinced that Lipiani was waiting for the situation to cool down, Salvatore greeted Tramontano as the farmer walked into his house.

"I've bought some beautiful land in Rome," beamed Tramontano as Maria dutifully kissed her husband.

"That's fantastic!" exclaimed Salvatore. "What do you plan to do with that land, live there?"

"Yes, we will build a large villa there and stay there for the rest of our lives," he said proudly as he put his arm around Maria's waist. "I understand that Michael and Bellaria were shot in a fight with the Gendarmes,"

"Yes. Michael was shot in the right arm."

"He must have had a nice sized hole," laughed Tramontano.

"That he does," responded Salvatore winking at Maria who instantly turned crimson. "He wants to avenge himself. Bellaria and Michael are planning to teach the Gendarmes a lesson."

"I wished he wouldn't do it," sighed Maria.

"You know Michael, nothing can stop him," chuckled Tramontano. "I'm surprised he hasn't gone already."

"He's waiting for Lipiani who was supposed to come-"

"Ah, that reminds me," said Tramontano, "I saw him in Enna. He said he would be here in the morning. I guess he didn't come because he feared that he would be followed or something like that. I really don't know, though."

In fact, that was indeed the case as the men discovered while talking to Lipiani the following day. Hearing the gunshots, Lipiani had fled to Enna where he awaited news of their status.

"In any case I have spoken to Baron Riccardi and he has agreed to meet you two on Friday," said Lipiani to Michael and Salvatore. "The situation looks promising for all of you," he said in a futile attempt to cheer up the men.

"What should we offer him?" asked Cangeliera feigning interest.

"Your protection. He isn't interested in having you eliminate other gangs; he just wants you around his properties to protect him from being robbed. Not a bad deal, huh?" said Lipiani with a beaming smile.

Thankful, the men offered Lipiani some money which he graciously accepted.

"We are truly fortunate to have such a good and wise friend," said Michael admiringly to Lipiani.

"Don't worry," chuckled Lipiani, "Someday I will need your help and I expect it."

"Surely," answered Michael.

Over lunch, Salvatore's futile attempt to convince

Bellaria and Michael not to return to Villarosa were disregarded.

"Sometimes, logic doesn't work, Salvatore. These men tried to humiliate us in our own villages! They must pay for their actions," Michael said as he and Bellaria set out towards Villarosa. "We will be back in the morning, I promise," said Michael, "Don't worry."

Bellaria and Michael rode most of the way in silence. Having decided upon a plan of action, the two men approached Villarosa from the south thereby bypassing the gendarme post on the northern end of the village.

Knowing the Gendarmes' habits, Michael and Bellaria decided to hide in the bell tower of the church in the main square. Opposite the church was a small bar where the Gendarmes were bound to be.

Moving quickly across the square, Michael smiled at Bellaria as they both recognized the Gendarmes' horses tied up outside the bar. Seeing that someone was coming, the two men ducked behind a large fountain, only to see the Mafioso Nardo La Verde, Santo Bellaria's uncle stroll by.

"Hey uncle!" whispered Bellaria. "Hey, over here."

The Mafioso, actually the head of the local mafia, walked over towards his nephew.

"What are you doing here?"

"We are laying a trap for the Gendarmes in there," said Michael pointing to the bar.

"They shot us several weeks ago. We're going to teach them a lesson - nothing drastic though," smiled Michael.

"Are you crazy? Everything that happens in this

village reflects upon me. When you robbed the granary, they held me for questioning for four days. No, please don't do anything. Please go away. They'll beat me and hold me responsible."

Michael and Bellaria looked at each other unhappily. After all, they didn't want to get Nardo La Verde in trouble, especially since he had often helped them in the past. But what of their vendetta?

After nearly half an hour of begging, Nardo La Verde was able to convince them not to do anything that he considered foolish.

"You are good men, you two," he said appreciatively as they unwillingly mounted their horses.

"I will owe you a very large favor. Hopefully I will be able to repay you soon," he said as he disappeared around the corner.

"Oh, well, so much for our vendetta," laughed Bellaria as he nudged his horse forward. "What are we going to tell the other men?"

"We will have to think of something," said Michael thinking that it probably turned out for the better. "You know, it's better this way."

"Yes. We could have gotten shot again," said Bellaria. "Can I ask you something? Didn't the bullet give you great pain?"

"What are you talking about?" laughed Michael.

"I mean, when you were shot, when Maria pulled the bullet out of your arm, you didn't even flinch. Didn't the pain drive you mad?" he asked sincerely.

"Yes," answered Michael.

"Yes, what?"

"Yes, it hurt," said Michael"

"Why didn't you scream then?"

"I don't know. I tried not to think about it."

"How is that possible? How could you stop yourself from screaming?"

"Maybe I'm getting used to it," answered Michael.

CHAPTER **TWELVE**

BARON RICCIARDI'S PROPERTY was immense. Besides the main estate, there were approximately twenty farm houses on the vast grounds that housed the farmers who worked the baron's land. Situated between two medium-sized mountains, the Ricciardi property spanned hundreds of acres in all directions.

The mid-morning sun was beginning to exude heat as Michael and Salvatore dismounted some three hundred yards before the main house. Walking their horses, they looked about at the baron's great wealth and thought about their possibilities of arranging a deal with Ricciardi.

When they were young, they both had worked for the baron, who was only two years their senior. As the baron was extremely fair and kind, Michael had enjoyed working for him. Somehow his personality and tact made the social distances between them seem insignificant. Often after working hours, Francesco Ricciardi had eaten with the boys. He had even invited them to catch eels with him one holiday.

Salvatore laughed aloud as he recalled how angry Michael had become when he put too much dynamite in the explosive in the eel pond.

"What are you laughing about?" asked Michael curiously.

"Oh nothing," Salvatore replied. "Do you remember the day we went eel hunting with the baron and you...?"

"Don't remind me," interjected Michael. "I put too much dynamite in the swamp and instead of killing the eels I blew the whole damn swamp apart."

Salvatore laughed heartily as he recalled Michael's burning face as the angry, thwarted eel hunter was converted with mud. What a temper, thought Salvatore.

"I wonder whether he will remember us. He was such a nice man, I think everything will work out," said Salvatore.

"Yes. Can you imagine how fantastic it would be just to hang around here all the time. Real rough, huh?" said Michael sarcastically.

"Let's hope for the best," said Salvatore as they approached the final twenty yards before the front door of Ricciardi's house.

Knocking softly on the large wooden door, Salvatore nervously recoiled his hand. Looking at Michael, Salvatore gesticulated a sign of hope to which Michael nervously smiled.

"Maybe you should knock again." said Michael after a few long tense moments.

As Salvatore was knocking, the thick door suddenly opened. A meticulously dressed butler answered the door requesting what their business was.

"We are supposed to meet Baron Ricciardi. I believe he is expecting us," stammered Salvatore.

Looking the two men carefully over, the butler nodded.

"I'll be right back. Wait here please," he said coolly as he closed the door.

"Well that was pretty strange," said Michael perplexed.

"Huh."

Walking around the corner of the house, Michael ran back to Salvatore.

"There are several black horses in the back!" he exclaimed excitedly.

"Something is not right here. Let's get out of here," said Salvatore as the door opened.

Looking at the men with obvious agitation, the butler asked them to please enter the house.

"We will be right back," said Michael as he turned around and began walking away from the house.

"Yes," muttered Salvatore, "We forgot something."

They hadn't walked fifteen frightening yards when they heard footsteps behind them.

"Halt!" ordered a voice.

Slowly turning to face the voice, Michael and Salvatore saw four Gendarmes facing them with their rifles out.

As sweat broke out on Salvatore's forehead, he observed Michael open his cloak to show the Gendarmes his hidden shotgun. Doing the same but fearing a confrontation, Salvatore racked his brain for a solution.

"What do you want from us?" asked Salvatore.

"You are both under arrest!" barked the corporal in charge.

"You aren't going to arrest anybody," said Michael coldly.

"Don't force us to use our weapons," replied the corporal.

"I'll tell you one thing, we may die today but I'm going to take some of you with me to hell," laughed Salvatore at the nervous Gendarmes.

The tension was becoming unbearable. Some moments Salvatore would think that he should start shooting, others that he should surrender. Not being sure that Michael wouldn't lose control and begin firing on the Gendarmes, Salvatore tried desperately to think of something that could end this encounter.

"Why don't you just go back into the house and leave us alone? We have families," said Salvatore.

"I'm not interested in either your family or your friends," snapped the corporal.

Friends, thought Salvatore. Of course, he could pretend that he had friends in the area!

"Well you are about to meet twenty of my friends," said Salvatore as he began whistling and waving for his supposed comrades who, naturally, were nowhere in the vicinity.

This bit of news set the corporal back. Slowly walking backwards, the four Gendarmes suddenly ran into the house, as Salvatore and Michael raced for their horses. Leaving at maximum speed, they headed :their horses towards the mountains that lay adjacent to the Ricciardi property. Knowing that they would soon be chased by the Gendarmes along with additional reinforcements, Salvatore and Michael hoped to gain a great distance between themselves and the Gendarmes.

It was nearly an hour later when they spotted a group of about twenty-five Gendarmes coming towards the mountain.

"Once we get off the mountain, we will be easy to spot," said Salvatore. "We should stay as close to them as possible so that we can see their every movement."

Agreeing, Michael led the way to a small cave where the two men hid their horses. Filling up the feed bags, they left the horses eating knowing that their preoccupation with food would keep them from making loud noises that could attract the Gendarmes.

For over eight hours, the Gendarmes searched the mountain, but to no avail. Finally, as darkness was beginning to wipe out any hope of finding the bandits, the Gendarmes regrouped and headed back towards Ricciardi's estate.

Making their way back to the horses took nearly two hours. Once they arrived, Salvatore decided that they should descend from the mountain on the opposite side. Agreeing, Michael began discussing the events of the day.

"Either Lipiani is a traitor or the baron is at fault. I think it's Lipiani," said Michael coldly.

"Yes, I agree, but we should give him a chance to explain. Maybe something went wrong. I-"

"Lipiani will come up with a good story. He's not stupid, you know," said Michael. "You know, now that I think about it, it was rather strange how we got ambushed in Villarosa. It was snowing and everyone was inside except those Gendarmes that just happened to be at the pasta factory. Lipiani is guilty, I'm sure of it."

"What I can't understand is why he would do such a thing? He surely doesn't need the money and-"

"Who knows? Who cares? All I know is that if he is guilty, he is a dead man," interjected Michael. "We placed our trust in him and he does this to us."

Worrying about the safety of their comrades, the two men rode in silence for the duration of the journey to Tramontane's farm. Stopping only once to eat, they finally arrived around mid-morning of the following day.

As they walked into the house, Lipiani's heart skipped a beat but he immediately collected his thoughts.

"How did it go then?" he asked calmly, convincingly.

"We were ambushed by four Gendarmes," answered Michael coolly.

"What!", exclaimed Lipiani faking anger and surprise perfectly.

"Yes, we were ambushed. Luckily we were able to get away unhurt," said Salvatore.

"Something must have gone wrong." stated Lipiani.

"Obviously," smiled Salvatore.

Looking at his watch, Lipiani got up to leave.

"I was planning on going to Enna, but I'll go see the baron first and let you know what happened," promised Lipiani.

"What's your rush?" asked Michael impatiently.

"I must be in Enna by morning. The Tramontane's had invited me to lunch, but I must leave now. I'm very concerned about the Ricciardi situation. We must find out what happened," said Lipiani, smiling to try to reassure the men.

As he was about to go out the door, Michael grabbed his arm.

"I just want you to know that if you betray us, you will die."

"What makes you say such a thing? How dare you insult me in this manner! I'm finished with all of you," shouted Lipiani.

"Michael, what have you done," said Salvatore. "Giorgio, please forgive him. He has gone through a great deal of misery lately and-"

"I'm sorry!" interjected Michael sheepishly. "I really am."

"You should be," said a stem-faced Salvatore as Lipiani, having graciously accepted all apologies, closed the door. They will all be dead soon, thought Lipiani nervously. Thank God for that!

Salvatore walked up to Santo Bellaria and handed him a shotgun.

"Follow him for at least four hours then come back," said Salvatore nonchalantly as he felt Michael's eyes piercing into the back of the head. Turning around, Salvatore smiled at his friend.

"I don't trust him either."

Michael laughed heartily.

"Aren't you clever", he asked sarcastically.

"We all do what we can," laughed Salvatore.

Maria had prepared a veritable feast. Pasta, lamb, cheese and wine were spread out all over the large table as the men sat down and ate.

"What a feast!" exclaimed Michael happily.

"It's not over yet," teased Maria as the squirming Michael tried to involve Tramontane in conversation.

"Well, what are you going to do?" asked Tramontane politely.

"I suppose we will try to offer some powerful man protection. If Lipiani is on the level, we will try to deal with Ricciardi: otherwise, we will seek out another man's riches that need protection", laughed Salvatore loudly as he attempted to drown out some of Maria's reckless remarks.

She was thoroughly happy. Her remarks were being understood by all the men, but she hardly cared. Salvatore, on the other hand, was desperately trying to keep Tramontane's attention hoping, even praying, that he wouldn't over hear one of Maria's comments.

Obviously aware of what Salvatore was doing, Maria decided that she could tease the nervous Salvatore.

"What are you two talking about?" she asked Salvatore loudly as her intoxicated state revealed itself via her eyes. "Michael and I are talking about-"

"Great food, huh men!" exclaimed Salvatore nervously and loudly. "How did you make it?"

"I cooked it," she laughed. "Don't you want to know what Michael and I were discussing? Salvatore, don't you?" she asked loudly as the room fell silent.

"I ... well ... I-"

"We were discussing," slurred Maria, "this thing that Michael has-"

"You don't know how lucky you are, Tramontane, to

have a wife that is such a tremendous cook," interrupted Salvatore as he attempted a nonchalant glare at Maria.

"Why are you looking at me that way?" she asked.

"Well, I'm ... I'm wondering why you don't eat your food. It's so delicious."

"The Gendarmes!" screamed Carmine Bellaria as he burst into the room.

"Lipiani met the Gendarmes on the road. They're coming here!" he screamed with panic written all over his face.

Salvatore quickly stood up and held his hands up thereby requesting calm and silence.

"Quickly get to your horses. Cangeliera, you and Michael gag the Tramontane's, this way they won't think you were accomplices. Hurry up men!"

The room burst with activity.

Worried, Michael tied Maria and then gagged her, telling her that he loved her, he stood up and walked quickly out the door. Five minutes after Carmine Bellaria's warning, the gang was galloping towards the forest. Swearing that he would have Lipiani's head, Michael, worried about Maria, led the group into the woods.

The group rode for nearly thirty minutes until they hit the outskirts of the woods. Moving quickly up the side of a large hill, they decided to stop and watch whatever action they could see from their binoculars; unfortunately they couldn't discern the events that would take place.

"We should have taken them with us," said Michael nervously.

They would have been accomplices then. This way

they will appear to have been our victims," said Salvatore, trying to reassure Michael as he desperately hoped that Lipiani hadn't relayed the true status of the situation.

After several moments of silence, Michael declared that he was going after Lipiani.

"We will go with you, Bellaria and I," said Cangeliera eagerly knowing that the golden moment had presented itself.

"I won't even try to stop you," said Salvatore calmly.

"Meet him at home in Enna. Obviously, the Ricciardi thing was a set up so he probably went home."

"We'll go straight to his home and pay him for his kindness," snickered Cangeliera maliciously.

"He's a dead man," said Michael trying to restrain his anger.

"We should leave soon," suggested Bellaria.

"Soon, we are leaving now!" ordered Michael as he found it intolerable to merely sit around and talk about Lipiani.

"Be careful, Michael," said Salvatore as he clasped his friend's hand.

"Aren't I always careful?" Michael laughed.

"Well, actually-"

"You don't have to answer that question," said Michael teasingly. "I know I'm a hot-head but I value my life more than you think."

Do you really?" Salvatore asked seriously.

Michael shrugged his shoulders and turned around. Patting Bellaria on the back, he walked quickly to his horse.

"Let's go. We are off to teach Lipiani a lesson he will never forget!" yelled Michael as Cangeliera and Bellaria mounted their horses.

Saluting Salvatore, Michael led Cangeliera and Bellaria out of the camp towards Enna as the Gendarmes approached the Tramontane farm.

Ordering his men to stop, and approach the house on foot, Pavesi dismounted.

"Surround the house and be quiet about it," he barked.

The young lieutenant approached the house slowly, guided by his ever increasing hatred for Cangeliera. Ever since old man Delvecchio had discovered that Cangeliera was a culprit, Pavesi had been unable to sleep. His rage and frustration had reached such intensity that he thought he was losing control of himself.

Quietly he peered into the window only to see Maria and her husband tied up on the floor.

"Shit!" muttered Pavesi under his breath as he kicked the door open. Startled, Maria jumped as she saw Pavesi's enraged, demonic expression.

"Corporal!" he yelled. "Corporal, get your ass in here!"

"Sir, where are-"

"Shut up! Lipiani, that slimy, stupid bastard must have been followed. In other words, corporal, the bandits are long gone!" he screamed loudly.

Trying to regain his composure he ordered the men to untie the petrified couple.

"Thank God you came to rescue us," gasped Tramontane. "We could have been here-"

"Shut your fat mouth!" barked Pavesi at the startled Tramontane.

"When did they leave?" he asked forcefully. "Was there a man named Cangeliera with them? Answer me!"

"I don't know their names. They left hours ago-" said Tramontane as Pavesi slammed his cane against Tramontane's face.

"My God, what is wrong with you!" screamed Tramontane painfully as he noticed Pavesi glaring at Maria.

"Do you think I'm stupid? Lipiani told me everything," he said hatefully as he approached the trembling Maria. Caressing her face, he barked at the corporal to take Tramontane out of the house.

"All of you get out!" he ordered over several chuckles from the men.

Silence weighed down the room.

"Do you know Cangeliera?" he asked calmly.

"Yes."

"Well, at least you are acting more intelligently than your husband. I can tell," he continued as he began stroking her face with the back of his hand, "that we will get along very well." Pavesi laughed.

"Please don't," she said forcefully as she moved her face away from his hand.

"Do you know," he said calmly as he began touching her lips with his fingers, "what he did to the girl that I love, that I am to marry in several weeks?" he pushed his index finger between her lips and into her mouth. Recoiling, she began crying while trembling uncontrollably.

"I had nothing to do with that ... please, leave me," she cried as he backed her up against the wall.

"She, my dear, was innocent too. Innocence has little to do with anything." he said as he began caressing her face with his open palm.

Moving his palm over her face towards her neck, he suddenly grabbed her long hair and yanked her to the ground. Dragging her on the ground towards the bedroom, he told her that he would show her what her friends were like.

Screaming wildly, she begged him to leave her as she held on to the bedroom door. Forcing her to let go of the door by kicking her hands, the crazed lieutenant threw her on the bed.

"Please, please," she pleaded as he pinned her legs under his. Slapping her several times, he began tying her hands on the brass bed posts,

"Don't ... please don't hit me," she screamed as he continued slapping her. "It wasn't my fault."

"Shut up you bitch!" he screamed as he tore off her blouse.

"Men," said the lieutenant as he walked out of the house buttoning his shirt, "have I got a beautiful surprise for you." Pavesi laughed crazily as the Gendarmes rushed into the house.

"You disgusting animal," screamed the tied-up Tramontane.

Lieutenant Pavesi pulled out his pistol and shot the poor farmer three times in the forehead.

Visibly trembling, Pavesi walked back into the house

and immediately headed for the table. Pouring a glass of wine, he immediately drank it down and repeated this ritual several times. Thirty minutes later, he was sound asleep on the table, dead drunk.

"Lieutenant," echoed a voice several hours later.

"What!" jumped Pavesi as he slowly recognized his corporal.

"I was just seeing if you were all right."

"Where are the men, still in there?" he asked pointing in the direction of the bedroom.

"No," laughed the corporal, "they can't-"

"All right corporal!" interrupted Pavesi, "Prepare them to leave, I'll be out soon," he mumbled as he stood up and stumbled towards Maria's room.

Completely naked, Maria was still tied to her bed crying incessantly. There were visible bite marks all over her abused body. And blood on her face from her broken nose. She turned her head to see Pavesi at the doorway. She laughed and cried as she recognized the lieutenant.

"Come for more, lieutenant?" she screamed.

"I wouldn't want to leave without a noteworthy farewell," he responded coldly.

"You bastard!" she screamed as he unbuckled his pants. By the time he had gotten on the bed, she had stopped crying. Staring up into his eyes, she revealed that intense Sicilian vengeful look that pierces one's soul.

"You know, Lieutenant, Cangeliera wasn't the only one who fucked your lover. They all did! Every last peasant did!" laughed Maria in hysterics.

"Stop it," he screamed as he punched her in the mouth.

"Lieutenant," she gasped.

"Don't say any more," he warned forcefully.

"Lieutenant?" she whispered.

"What is it!" he exclaimed loudly.

"I told your men!" she suddenly screamed as she began laughing wildly.

"No!" Pavesi screamed in agony as he strangled the life out of Maria Tramontane.

CHAPTER **THIRTEEN**

HAVING TRAVELLED ALL night, Michael, Bellaria, and Cangeliera were greeted by the simultaneous appearance of the large orange sun and the village of Enna on the horizon. Tired and irritable, the men proceeded towards their destination in silence.

Enna was larger than Villarosa. Lipiani lived in Pasquasia, a fairly rural environment. Fortunately, his home was situated between their present position and the center of town.

The sun climbed rapidly upwards as its color changed from a deep orange to a brilliant gold and finally found its normal state in a washed out yellowish tone. Cool early morning breezes were rapidly warmed and transformed into dry still air. Sicily's sun was very intense, ever present, ever powerful.

The light blue cheerful sky contrasted sharply with their moods as the men approached Lipiani's villa. Lipiani's home was a large, unpretentious affair that exuded wealth of a modest degree combined with an earthy common sense that smeared its common way through every crack of the villa. Surrounded by many fruit trees, the garden offered its users often needed protection from the harshness of the sun.

Michael dismounted and tied his horse to a tree.

Following him in the house, Santo Bellaria and Cangeliera looked nervously about them. A small boy greeted the men as they entered Lipiani's home.

"Hi!" exclaimed the boy cheerfully.

"Hello," responded Michael slowly. "We are looking for Giorgio Lipiani-"

"My uncle is in the back. You can go around the house and walk straight back and go over the hill. It's pretty far so you may want to take your horses."

"Thank you," said Michael sadly; he felt badly for the cheerful boy. Such is life, though, he thought.

Walking back to their horses, the men mounted and began moving towards the direction that the boy was pointing to. Waving goodbye to the men, the boy ran back to the house to continue playing.

The heat was becoming unbearable. Removing their cloaks, then their shirts, the men complained nervously about' the heat. The sweet smell of various fruits reached their nostrils and Michael realized how hungry he was. Leaning over, he grabbed a few figs from the tree and began to eat them. Silently, they proceeded onwards.

Lipiani's property was full of fruit trees, vegetables, and various spices and herbs. The mixture of the sweet smell of various fruits combined with the earthy crisp smell of rosemary reminded Michael of Franco's garden.

Franco had, in fact, been the one to introduce Michael and Salvatore to Lipiani. It was a cool February day when they had first met the nervous bejeweled Mafioso. Speaking very kind words to them, he had offered them his help in a rather ticklish situation.

After Michael had totally destroyed Franco Di Meglio's carriage, the merchant from Palermo had decided to take the matter to the courts. Knowing that Michael would certainly be incarcerated, Franco had requested Lipiani's help. A brief visit to Palermo by a good friend of Lipiani's had convinced the merchant to drop the matter.

"Ah, there you are," Lipiani had said to Michael and Franco several days later. "The case has been dismissed. Di Meglio withdrew his statement."

Jumping for joy, Michael thanked Lipiani incessantly.

"No need to thank me," he said. "You will repay." Repay he did.

About two years later, Michael, coming home exhausted from work, was greeted by Lipiani who, seated at the table sipping wine, requested Michael to join him. Michael knew why he was there.

"How are you Don Lipiani?" he asked nervously.

"Fine. Just fine."

"What can I do for you?"

"Well, I'm glad you asked. I have this friend who has a very lovely daughter. Well, one day when she was walking back from school, two boys, about eighteen years old, approached her and bothered her. Nothing serious, you understand. They just grabbed her breast and and tried to pull up her dress. You know," he had said while pouring a glass of wine, "the usual kid's stuff."

Lipiani took a long gulp of the red wine, then continued, "You see, Michael, she doesn't have an older brother nor is her father in good health. You can see why I immediately thought of you. Michael would understand her father's despair, I thought to myself."

"What would you have me do?" Michael had asked nervously.

"Teach those boys a small lesson, that's all. And Michael, do it in public so to put fear into the other boys with similar ideas."

"Who are these people?" Michael has asked anxiously.

"I'm afraid I don't know who the boys are, but the girl's name is Rosalia Ansalone. Lovely girl, terribly shy, though."

Lipiani had smiled as Michael recalled the two or three times he had seen the girl in question as she had shyly looked at him.

"Rosalia Ansalone." Michael had smiled.

"You know her?"

"Oh, I've seen her here and there a couple of times. She's very pretty but, you are right Don Lipiani, she is very shy."

"Well, I must be off. Try to find out who these boys are in a discreet manner. Don't involve the girl. If you must, ask her father, but I prefer that you don't-."

"I have friends at her school," Michael had responded, thinking of Franco. "I'm sure I can find out."

"It is agreed then?"

"Yes."

"Good," Lipiani had said as he was preparing to leave. "You are an honorable man, Michael Moccia."

Through Franco, Michael had discovered that the boys were Cangeliera and Santo Bellaria who, at the time, were unknown to Michael.

About two weeks after Lipiani's visit, Michael was waiting outside of a bar for Franco when he saw Rosalia followed by the two boys in question. Obviously saying nasty things to her, the boys crossed the town square chuckling. Winking at Franco, Michael had walked across the square.

"Hey you!" he screamed ferociously faking anger as Rosalia looked at him.

"You two, come here!" Michael had barked at the petrified duo£ as they walked nervously towards him.

Even though Michael was only three years older than the boys, his size, and obvious incredible strength differentiated him from them.

That mild February afternoon, Michael had soundly thrashed the petrified boys in the presence of an adoring Rosalia - who later turned out to be his wife.

Life is strange, thought Michael as he looked at Bellaria and Cangeliera and recalled how they cried that day in February; now they were going to kill Lipiani. Michael wondered whether Bellaria and Cangeliera knew that Lipiani had been behind their humiliation. He doubted it.

He thought again about that day so long ago.

After having completed his punitive task, Michael had walked over to Rosalia.

"They won't bother you again."

"You did this for me?" she had said looking up into his eyes.

"Well, I certainly didn't do it for my grandmother."

"Why?"

"I saw a lovely girl in distress and I thought–"

"You think I'm lovely!" she exclaimed as if she thought that she was a monster.

"Why, yes. Isn't it obvious?"

"No," she said as she began walking away.

"Wait a minute," Michael had said walking after her. "May I walk with you?"

"Yes, of course," she said annoyed at herself for having revealed too much enthusiasm.

"What is your name?" he said feigning ignorance.

"Rosalia. Rosalia Ansalone. I know yours."

"How's that?"

"Everyone knows you."

"If you say so," he had laughed.

The following day Michael had met her outside of the school. Pleasantly surprised, she looked nervously about. She hoped that all would see who was waiting for her.

"Hi."

"Hello. You know my father says you are a real good man."

"What does that mean?"

"I don't know. He doesn't say that about many people. I thought you would be pleased–"

"Oh, I am. I am," responded Michael smiling.

Their conservation continued aimlessly as he walked her home.

"Why do you study?"

"To better myself," she answered curtly.

"Do you really think-"

"Yes, I do," she interrupted. "I think we should all try to better ourselves, don't you?"

"Well, let me ask you something. What do they teach you to do when you want to do something, but you are afraid that someone will be offended by your gesture?"

"What are you babbling about?" she asked totally confused.

"Suppose you wanted to do something. If you thought the thing you wanted to do might offend somebody that you cared about, what would you do?"

"Are your intentions honorable in this case?"

"Yes, they would be."

"Well, then, do it and if the person has any brains, they will understand."

"This person has brains," Michael has said as he turned Rosalia around and kissed her. He never forgot the look on her face.

Lipiani was inspecting some leaves as the three men rode up to him. Slowly turning around, he blinked nervously under the hot mid-morning sun as he recognized the three men. Sighing, he dropped his shovel and shrugged his shoulders as if indicating that there was nothing he could do.

"Come on," he screeched, "get it over with."

"Why did you betray us?" asked Michael softly. "What reason could you have had?"

"What difference does it make?"

Nodding, and thereby acknowledging Lipiani's statement, Michael looked up at the sun, then back to

Lipiani. Wet from the heat, the white hairs that were sprinkled about Lipiani's hair began to soften. Lipiani, pulling some grapes out of a sack, began eating them as if unconcerned by the presence of these three men who were about to kill him. That was destiny, thought Giorgio Lipiani.

Michael breathed deeply then swiftly pulled out his shotgun and blasted Lipiani's chest wide open.

"Let's go," he ordered solemnly as Lipiani's body jerked for the final time.

Galloping at full speed, then men raced for the house. When they went by it, they saw the startled boy run out of the house and look at them; he suddenly ran in the direction of his uncle.

The three men continued at a rapid pace for several hours. By noon, they had reached a semi-protected valley where they decided to rest and eat.

"We are going to Villarosa to see our families," explained Bellaria. "What are you going to do, Michael?"

"I'll accompany you to the outskirts of town, but then I'll move on to the Tramontane farm," he said, wondering about what might have happened there.

"I'd be careful if I were you. The Gendarmes are bound to know Lipiani was killed. We will certainly be suspected," warned Michael.

"Yes, he is right," said Bellaria nervously. "Maybe we shouldn't go home. They will probably be waiting for us."

"Nonsense," snapped Cangeliera. "They would never dream that we would go home now. Who could do such a thing? We would!" He laughed heartily as Michael and

Bellaria joined him.

"It's too bad about the boy, though," said Michael thoughtfully. "He is young and innocent. It will be a great shock to him, I'm sure."

"Yes, but he must grow up sometime. It might as well be now," said Bellaria, not really meaning what he said.

"I guess so."

"Hey! Let's go!" exclaimed Cangeliera cheerfully. "We don't want the Gendarmes to shoot us while we are eating, do we?"

It took them several more hours before they reached the outskirts of Villarosa. The mid-afternoon sun was relentlessly beating down on the men as they stopped to bid each other farewell,

"I'll see you both at Tramontane's in two days," said Michael.

"Yes," said Bellaria.

"No", contradicted Cangeliera.

Turning his head towards Cangeliera, Michael saw the shotgun pointed at him. Smiling, he instantly thought of Lipiani and how he must have felt before he died.

Michael's life seemed to flash before his eyes. Rosalia and children, his childhood with Franco and Salvatore, Maria and Grazia - but inwardly, Michael was calm and almost happy that he was going to die. The long string of misery would finally be cut. All would be forgotten and he, Michael Moccia, would finally be at peace.

Cangeliera must detest me, thought Michael. Hoping to be able to shoot him, Michael attempted to stall Cangeliera.

"What does this mean?"

"You are going to die, my friend."

Looking at Bellaria incredulously, Michael said, "You are in this too, Santo?"

Bellaria nodded apologetically.

"Why?"

"You ask too many questions," snapped Cangeliera.

"Don't I have a right to know why I'm going to die?" asked Michael as he slowly moved his hand towards his gun.

"Dying men have no rights," snapped Cangeliera.

Unbearably long moments of tension were finally broken when Michael went for his gun. As he was pulling his gun from under his cloak, Cangeliera shot him in the face. Flying off his petrified horse, Michael clutched his face in agony as Cangeliera and Bellaria shot him several more times.

For several minutes, Bellaria and Cangeliera stared at the lifeless body of Michael Moccia as if expecting him to stand and shoot them. The bright afternoon sun glared down at them harshly, even pitifully. An eerie silence spread its thick wings over the morbid landscape.

"We'll wait for nightfall, and then we'll bury him," said Cangeliera.

"Where?" asked Bellaria tearfully.

"In the graveyard," smiled Cangeliera. His expression quickly changed upon seeing that Bellaria was neither amused nor impressed with his idea.

Bellaria dismounted and pulled a blanket off of his horse.

Draping the blanket over Michael's blood-stained body, he shuddered.

"Why are you so afraid? He's dead!" exclaimed Cangeliera arrogantly. "He can't do you any harm. Do you understand, he's dead?"

Nodding, obviously not wanting to discuss the matter, Bellaria walked over to a tree and sat down in the shade. Rolling a cigarette, Bellaria continued to tremble as Cangeliera walked over to him.

"Michael Moccia didn't rape anyone," Bellaria said calmly. "You know that didn't you?"

"What are you talking about? Have you gone mad?"

"Maybe," he said sullenly.

"Listen," began Cangeliera, "You are in this up to your ears. Don't try to blame anything on-"

"Shut up!" screamed Bellaria at the shocked Cangeliera who had never witnessed such a response from his friend. "Just leave me alone."

Cangeliera sat down and awaited the darkness.

As soon as it was deemed dark enough, the two men hoisted Michael onto his horse and began making their way towards the Villarosa graveyard which was situated between the main square and the chapel. Though it was an odd location for a cemetery, the people of Villarosa prided themselves in its simple beauty and its functional nature.

Several hundred years old, the cemetery was completely surrounded by a high brick wall. The only entrance was by the guard house, which, for obvious reasons, Cangeliera and Bellaria decided to avoid.

Actually, Cangeliera thought that the concept of

burying Michael in the cemetery was extraordinarily clever. Who, he surmised, could ever guess that he would be buried there? What genius, thought Cangeliera as he glanced unpleasantly up the ten foot high wall that he had to hoist Michael over and then scale.

"How in the hell are we supposed to get him over that!" said Bellaria incredulously as he looked from Michael's body to the wall.

"Stand up on your horse and get on top of the wall. I'll hand him to you and you'll-"

"Are you crazy?" How are you going to hand-"

"Wait! I have an idea. Get on the other side and I'll tie a rope around his chest under his arms; then you can pull him u p and let him drop over," said Cangeliera with real excitement.

"That's better," said Bellaria.

Presently he stood up on his horse and easily jumped over the wall by aiding himself with his hands. Falling hard on the other side, Bellaria let out a small scream to which Cangeliera reacted severely.

Cangeliera pulled a long rope from his saddlebag and headed towards Michael's body. Yanking him off the horse, Cangeliera wrapped the rope under Michael's arms, then the two ends over the wall.

Grabbing the two ends, Bellaria sat down on the ground and propped his legs against the wall at a slight angle, upwards. Using his back and legs, he pulled Michael's body to the top of the wall. Quickly moving out of the way, he signaled audibly to Cangeliera to push the body over. Cangeliera quickly followed.

Walking over to the first grave, Cangeliera pointed at the large stone covering that the two men were to move.

"You want to just throw him in the grave?" asked Bellaria.

"What else? Come, give me a hand. This damn thing must weigh a ton."

For nearly twenty minutes, the two sweating, panting men pushed the stone which finally came loose enough to be able to fit Michael's body in the grave.

"Come on," said Cangeliera excitedly. "Let's drag him in here."

Running over to the body, they each placed one arm around their neck and dragged him into the grave. Once pushing inside, they again wrestled with the large stone. It finally moved into place - not, however, without making a loud screaming sound.

"Who goes there?" yelled a voice some three hundred feet from them.

Running to the wall, they helped each other over, Bellaria climbing on Cangeliera's back, then Santo pulling Cangeliera up the wall. Cangeliera let out a loud scream and immediately began clutching his right leg.

"It's broken!" he exaggerated.

Be quiet," ordered Bellaria as he heard the guard approaching the wall from the other side.

Bellaria helped Cangeliera onto his horse, and then mounted his own. Quickly, the men galloped away into the night.

Giovanni Mosumecci, the guard at the cemetery, had rushed over to the spot where the loud crashing noise had come from. Hearing several horses galloping, he saw the cracked cover of Signora Puntieri's grave. Suspecting some criminal act, he immediately headed for the Gendarme's station in Villarosa.

"Corporal Vesce!" he said knocking on the station's door. "Corporal Vesce, open the door, quickly!"

"What is it?" asked the annoyed corporal upon seeing Mosumecci. "What do you want?"

"Something strange has happened at the cemetery tonight," replied the excited guard.

"Did you see a ghost?" laughed the corporal as he turned his head to see who had joined his laughter.

"No, no, seriously. I heard a crashing noise and-"

"Drinking again?" asked a laughing voice from inside the station.

"Won't you listen to me?" asked Mosumecci angrily.

"Yes, yes. Come in," said the bored corporal. "What did you hear?" he asked nonchalantly as he sat down at his desk.

"Well, as I said, I heard a loud noise. When I investigated, I heard some horses galloping away and I noticed that one of the graves, Signora Puntieri's grave, may she rest in-"

"Get to the point," barked the tired corporal.

"... Was broken," said the guard.

"What was broken?"

"The cover of the grave."

"The cover?" asked the corporal perplexed.

"Yes, as if someone had dropped it," said the guard, playing detective.

"I wonder what ... well, let's take a look, shall we?" he said as he motioned for two of his men to follow him.

"Did you get a chance to see the men?" asked the corporal as he walked out of the station.

"No. They were already on the other side of the wall. You see, I foolishly yelled out when I heard the noise. I-"

"It's all right," snapped the corporal.

All four men struggled with the heavy stone for several minutes. When they were able to remove it, the guard gasped at the sight of Michael's battered body. The men wrestled with Michael's body until they finally got it out of the grave.

'Who is it I wonder?" said the corporal.

"I have no idea," answered the guard.

The following morning Grazia Campo heard a loud knock on her front door. Walking quickly to answer it, she was slightly disappointed when Angelina greeted her. Not that she didn't adore Angelina, but every knock on the door could be Salvatore and when it turned out to be someone she saw often, well, she would become depressed, just slightly.

"Have you heard?" Angelina asked excitedly.

"Heard what?"

"Last night they found an extra body in one of the graves, in Maria Puntieri's grave, in fact," chuckled Angelina. "Anyway, we are all supposed to go by the cemetery and see if we can identify who it is,"

Grazia turned white.

"Don't be silly, Grazia, it's not Salvatore!"

"I know, but I always think that he may end up dead

someday. I don't know what I'd do-"

"Oh stop it! Let's go see. Come on, let's go," she said anxiously. Slowly preparing for the short journey, Grazia asked Angelina how she had heard of this.

"I was in town this morning. Everyone was talking about it. The square was packed, you wouldn't believe it!"

"I bet," said Grazia thinking how morbid most people are. "All right, I'm ready."

Closing the door of her house, she continued her animated discussion with Angelina until they entered the main square. Packed with humanity, the loud square was bustling with speculation. It seemed that nearly everyone was attempting to guess who the victim might be, but no one knew because of the incredible disfiguration that the shotgun had carved in Michael's body.

"Shall we take a look?" asked Angelina, visibly excited.

"Yes, I suppose so," smiled Grazia, thinking how funny Angelina looked when she was excited, let's leave."

"I can't stand this dying anymore!" Grazia screamed.

Walking towards the center of attention, Grazia thought that she had seen everyone in Villarosa in the square. Inside the cemetery on a large slab of cement lay a man.

Instantly she recognized him. The large muscles on his arms and legs, the many unique peculiarities all over his body were unmistakable to his sister. As she began trembling, Angelina asked, "What's wrong? Who is it?"

"Michael," she whispered as she burst into tears. Suddenly the entire square seemed to go silent as Grazia's cry drowned out all the idle chatter and speculation.

She walked over to his body and forced herself to look at his destroyed face. Her deep sorrow could only be matched by the intense hatred she felt for the culprits, whoever they may be.

Who would do such a thing? Why kill Michael? It had to be a scoundrel who shot him while he wasn't expecting it, she thought. No man would face Michael in a fair fight. But nothing was fair and he knew that best of all.

She wondered about Salvatore and whether he was dead also. After all, Michael and Salvatore were inseparable. If one was dead, wouldn't it be logical to assume that the other might be also dead? Not only possible, but probable, she thought.

"What pigs could have done such a thing?" she whispered deliriously. "Why him?"

"Why don't we go home," said Angelina crying. "Please, Grazia, let's leave."

"I can't stand this dying anymore!" Grazia screamed. "Where is my husband? Is he lying in some gutter, butchered by other bandits or by the Gendarmes? Are we always going to live amidst all this death?" she cried as Angelina walked her out of the cemetery.

It took several hours to get to the Campo home, for Grazia constantly stopped and began crying. Finally, however, she arrived at her house.

Not knowing where her husband was, whether he was dead or alive, the lonely Grazia wept over her brother's death and wished that she too would die.

CHAPTER **FOURTEEN**

"CAREFUL!" YELLED CANGELIERA in obvious pain as Bellaria helped him off his horse.

"I'm trying to do the best I can", apologized Bellaria, while Cangeliera sat on the ground rubbing his leg.

Nearly four hours they had ridden since they had left Michael in the grave. Cangeliera, though complaining loudly of his injury, insisted on moving ahead for fear of being chased by the Gendarmes.

"Don't worry!" exclaimed Bellaria in response to Cangeliera's agitated expression. "They have no idea who did it. We have absolutely nothing to worry about."

"For now," responded Cangeliera. "It won't take Salvatore too long to figure out what happened once news of Michael's death reaches him. I think we should leave Sicily."

"Yes, I suppose we must," said Bellaria sadly. "We'll go get the money from Delvecchio and leave as fast as possible. In a year, we should be able to come back with our amnesty."

"You'll go to Delvecchio alone," said Cangeliera, thinking that his daughter may be well enough to recognize him. Cangeliera grabbed and rubbed his leg. "My leg, I'll just slow us down. You understand, don't you?"

"Well, yes, but where will you go?" asked the reluctant Bellaria, thinking about the trip he would have to make alone.

"My cousin has a small house in Caltanissetta. We'll go there together so that you'll know where to meet me. It shouldn't take more than eight hours at the most," said Cangeliera carefully. "We'll go to the mainland. They'll never catch us there!"

Nodding in approval, Bellaria indicated that they should begin their trip to Cangeliera's cousin's house. Feeling anxious about leaving Sicily, Bellaria thought about the many cruel situations that nature had presented him with. Now, he thought, he was a murderer forced to leave his home by circumstance, by chance, and by an apathetic genre of greed that he didn't fully understand. Knowing that Michael had been innocent, Bellaria had chosen to think that he believed in Michael's guilt, but in reality, the lure of money and amnesty had forced his hand. In a sense, Bellaria attempted to disbelieve the fact that his lucid mind was well aware of the true circumstances that had recently surrounded his existence.

"May I ask you a sincere question?" he asked Cangeliera calmly as they were walking their way to the cousin's house.

"Well ... yeah, sure!" laughed Cangeliera uncertainly.

"I mean will you answer me honestly?"

"Yes!" said Cangeliera faking annoyance.

"Did you rape Marina Delvecchio?" asked Bellaria as he gazed at Cangeliera with heretofore unseen intensity.

"Yes."

Bellaria sighed out of a combination of anger, despair, and relief. Relief was a sensation that was attributable to Bellaria's confirmation of his former beliefs. Feeling tricked, then frustrated and angry Bellaria remained silent for a long period of time.

When they finally approached the house, Bellaria, indicating that he was leaving, turned his horse around and set out for Delvecchio's estate.

"Are you coming back?" asked Cangeliera anxiously as his friend headed east.

Bellaria failed to answer, but Cangeliera felt sure that his friend would come for him. After all, he was an accomplice in a murder; it was too late for remorse. The money and the freedom they would soon receive would aid the smoothing out of their relationship, thought Cangeliera as Bellaria disappeared behind some trees. Too much had happened to be able to look back. Only the future counted, the past would only exist in books and in faded memories that would soften with age.

By the time Bellaria reached the Delvecchio estate, Lieutenant Pavesi was a physical, emotional and spiritual wreck. Not having slept for what appeared to be weeks, Pavesi's mind had not stopped thinking of Cangeliera for more than a few hours. The passion that had developed in his soul, the hatred for the individual that had tampered with Pavesi's spiritual Utopia had gone beyond the normal into an almost schizophrenic admiration-detestation condition.

Delvecchio was not in a much different state. Marina's condition had been severely set back due to her having seen the terrifying presence of Cangeliera. Having sent his daughter to Milano for treatment, Delvecchio vowed that he would have Cangeliera's head.

For several days, the two men waited in an ominous silence that resembled a storm that was about to unleash its furious temper upon the landscape. News of Michael's death had reached them; their expectations were brimming, ready to explode within a moment's notice. Assuming that Cangeliera suspected nothing of their newly-acquired knowledge, the two men had agreed that Cangeliera would seek out his rewards; and so they waited as cats wait for their prey.

A soft knock on the door quickened the pulses of the lieutenant and the baron. Opening the door to a fatigued Bellaria, Pavesi looked about Bellaria in an attempt to spot Cangeliera.

"He couldn't make it," said Bellaria matter-of-factly. "There was an accident ... he broke his leg. Anyway, Moccia is dead."

"Come in, uh ... what was your name?"

"Santo. Santo Bellaria."

Oh yes. Bellaria, of course. Sit down, please" said Pavesi, still ruffled by Cangeliera's absence.

"Hello, Baron. How are you sir?" asked Bellaria amiably.

"He broke his-"

"Where is he?" screamed the lieutenant, startling Bellaria.

"I don't know..."

"Liar!" screamed Pavesi as he walked up to Bellaria

and slapped him hard across the face.

Immediately, Bellaria jumped to his feet ready to retaliate, when four Gendarmes entered the room pointing their rifles at Bellaria. Pushing Bellaria back down in his chair, Pavesi began pacing the room screaming that Bellaria would die if he didn't reveal Cangeliera's location.

"What is wrong with you?" asked Bellaria pretending ignorance. "We had an agreement and now ... now you threaten me ... What's so important about Cangeliera?" he asked.

"Cangeliera? Cangeliera is a dead man!" screamed Delvecchio as he pounded the arm of the chair. "Don't play games with me, you know what he did. I'll have your balls on the table if you don't talk!"

Truly frightened but still wanting to have Delvecchio and, especially, Pavesi believe in his ignorance in the matter, Bellaria reiterated his question regarding Cangeliera.

"Don't play games!" exclaimed Pavesi loudly as he slapped Bellaria on the face several times.

Bellaria's fright turned to anger as the stinging slaps struck his face. Pushing Pavesi away from him, he stood up as if he were about to attack the crazed lieutenant. Four Gendarmes grabbed him and yanked him up against the wall.

Walking slowly towards the trembling Bellaria, Pavesi looked like a wild bull attacking his pursuers. Opening his hand, Pavesi slapped Bellaria in the groin with the back of his hand. As Bellaria bent over in pain, Pavesi punched him hard on the jaw.

Bleeding profusely, the moaning Bellaria cursed the

lieutenant. That generated a frenzy of beatings from all the Gendarmes, whose experience and practice had made them enamored with the infliction of pain on individuals.

"Stop!" screamed Pavesi, recalling the Spilatieri incident. "We want him very much alive, don't we Bellaria?"

Rising from his chair, Delvecchio walked over to Bellaria and stood over the battered prisoner.

"You are going to tell us or else I'll have you tortured. You do have a family, don't you?" asked Delvecchio in an evil tone.

"You son of a-" started Bellaria who was immediately silenced by a hard kick in the ribs.

Leaning over to look directly into Bellaria's eyes, Delvecchio's intensity was unmistakable.

"Listen you son of a bitch, I'll send these men to visit your wife, daughters, son's mother I guarantee you that what they will do won't be pleasant. These men are lonely and-"

"Stop it!" pleaded Bellaria who presently began crying. "Leave my family alone!" You understand?"

"Tell me where he is! Tell me now or-" Pavesi suddenly slapped Bellaria hard on the face. "Tell us!" screamed Pavesi.

"I'll ... I ... I can't, " said Bellaria softly as Delvecchio calmly straightened out his body.

"Corporal," ordered the lieutenant. "Take five men and visit the Bellaria home," he barked eyeing Bellaria. "Rape all the women, disfigure them and kill everyone when you are finished."

"Stop! I'll do it, stop them," pleaded Bellaria as Pavesi

motioned to the corporal to disregard his orders.

"Well, where is he?" asked Delvecchio impatiently.

"About four miles from Caltanissetta, four miles due east, you'll find him in a small house in the bottom of a small valley. He'll be there! Stop those men!" he yelled pointing to the corporal.

"Don't worry," smiled Pavesi triumphantly. "They aren't going anywhere. Don't worry." He laughed.

"We are all going to visit your wife," said Delvecchio calmly.

"What?" screamed Bellaria, as Pavesi gave Delvecchio a puzzled look.

"You promised-" said Bellaria.

"Shut up!" snapped Delvecchio. "It's just an insurance to make sure that you are not lying. Nothing will happen to her unless-"

"Brilliant!" exclaimed Pavesi admiringly. "Absolutely brilliant."

Visibly angry, Bellaria felt completely trapped in the present circumstances. Realizing that he would soon have to face his wife and children, his shame encompassed his entire essence. Cangeliera's greed, his cruelty had been the cause of everyone's troubles; Bellaria began to hate the man with a rarely seen passion.

Naturally, Delvecchio knew this and was using it to his advantage. Feeling sure that Bellaria had indeed told the truth, Delvecchio and Pavesi decided to leave for Villarosa to get Bellaria's wife and then continue to Cangeliera's location. Being essentially on the way to Caltanissetta, Villarosa would present only a minor detour to the impatient men.

"Tell me something," said Delvecchio as the men were preparing for the journey to Villarosa. "Why did you kill Moccia when you knew that he was innocent? We both knew that he was an honest man."

"I don't know ... I think ... I suppose it was for the promise of wealth and amnesty. How did you find out?" he asked sadly.

Delvecchio was silent for a few minutes. Thinking about his daughter, he looked sternly at Bellaria. "Last time he was here ... she saw him ... he left quickly."

Nodding, Bellaria followed the lieutenant out of the room towards the horses.

"I'm going to kill that bastard," said Pavesi calmly as he mounted his horse.

Silently, Bellaria wished the same.

By the time the party reached the gendarme's station in Villarosa, the entire village was aware of Bellaria's capture and his involvement in Michael's murder. Unable to look at anyone out of shame, Bellaria stared at the ground as he was escorted into the station. There he waited for his wife.

Some forty minutes later, she walked into the station flanked on both sides by several Gendarmes. Frightened and ashamed, she immediately burst into tears as she ran up to Bellaria and hugged him.

"What have you done?" she whispered anxiously.

Bellaria, thoroughly humiliated, began crying hysterically as she attempted to soothe the pain.

"Enough of the crap!" barked Pavesi loudly. "We'll

be leaving in an hour and Bellaria, you better be right or I shall enjoy-" said Pavesi gesturing to Bellaria's petrified wife.

"Don't you worry," yelled Bellaria, "Cangeliera is as good as dead!"

"Good. You see, Baron, he is a reasonable man," laughed Pavesi at the doubtful Delvecchio.

Gesturing to Pavesi to come closer, Delvecchio whispered, don't forget that he is Sicilian."

"He is human," laughed Pavesi. "No difference, no difference at all."

Pavesi's laughter was interrupted by loud voices emanating from outside the station's door. Pavesi opened the door only to be greeted by an influx of some twenty agitated women.

Literally pushing Pavesi aside, the screaming women stormed into the station and made their way straight for Bellaria, who suddenly became quite alarmed seeing the horde of women approaching him. Talking all at once, they began shouting at the confused Bellaria; he looked helplessly at the amused Pavesi for guidance.

Pavesi indicated to a guard to shoot in the air which obviously silenced the room immediately.

"Ladies, please state your business with my prisoner and please," he continued raising his right hand thereby requesting not to be interrupted, "don't talk all at once."

"We want to know where our husbands are!" screamed a woman who appeared to have the temperament to attack Bellaria at any moment.

"What?" asked Bellaria totally confused.

"Where are our husbands?" she reiterated. "What have you done with them, you murderer!"

"I don't know what you are talking about," said Bellaria sincerely.

"You better find out soon," laughed Delvecchio.

"Hell hath no fury," stated Pavesi.

"We know you went to school, lieutenant! Let's get this matter cleared up and go after Cangeliera," said Delvecchio with irritation.

"All right ladies, explain yourselves. Who are your husbands and what connections exist between him and them?" said Pavesi pointing at Bellaria.

"They all rode together. When we heard that Michael Moccia was found in the graveyard, we feared for their lives. Now that the murderer is here, he should know something," said an excited young woman whose face revealed nothing but anxiety. "What did you do with Mario?" she asked addressing Bellaria.

"I don't know where he is," said Bellaria coolly. "Nor do I care where he is!"

"You liar - you murdered," yelled one of the many.

"You and Cangeliera probably killed them all and put their bodies in-"

"The cemetery!" screamed a voice from the crowd.

"Are they in the cemetery?" asked the young woman loudly.

"Yeah, sure," said Bellaria sarcastically as he realized that he would be blamed for all the deaths, even though he had only killed Michael.

Naturally, his tone was neither appreciated nor

understood; Pavesi's statement that Bellaria hadn't meant what he said was drowned out by the mob of excited women who rushed out of the door and raced for the cemetery.

A large crowd finally arrived at the cemetery and swarmed over the graves. Uncovering every grave in sight, the crowd worked furiously for several hours. Suddenly a loud scream brought the entire crew over to a large grave. Some eight fresh bodies were piled into the grave.

Though none of the bodies was recognized by anyone, their mere presence generated hysteria in the crowd. Everyone marched toward the station.

Hearing the loud crowd approaching the station, Pavesi ordered all his men outside to stop the mob's forward progress. Threatening to open fire, the Gendarmes were able to hold the screaming, angry crowd back, but barely.

Being informed of the situation, Pavesi assured the ladies of the mob that justice would prevail. Bellaria would be punished, but he was necessary to apprehend his partner in crime, Cangeliera, assured Pavesi.

"We want him now!" screamed an elderly man.

"You can't! He is our prisoner and will remain thus. Any attempt to interfere with the law will be severely and instantly squashed!" responded Pavesi angrily as he joined Delvecchio in walking back into the gendarme station. There he found Santo Bellaria with his wrists slashed. He was dead.

Delvecchio put his hand on Pavesi's shoulder. "No difference, huh?"

CHAPTER **FIFTEEN**

BY THE TIME the Gendarmes left the Tramontane estate, Salvatore was extremely nervous. Dawn was just beginning to shoot its unwanted light across the valley. The early morning chill had seeped its numbing claws into Salvatore's bones.

All night the Gendarmes had remained at Tramontane's. Although from Salvatore's vantage point he could neither hear nor see anything detailed, the prolonged presence of the Gendarmes worried him.

Squinting as the first sun rays pierced his tired eyes, Salvatore walked over to the other men.

"I think I'm going to see what happened," he said, trembling from the cold.

"When will you be back?" asked Carmine Bellaria.

"Soon, I'll be back in two or three hours. In fact, if I'm not back by then, come down to the farm. Agreed?" asked Salvatore nervously looking in the direction of the farm.

Thinking that Michael, Cangeliera, and Bellaria must 'be well on their way to Enna, Salvatore mounted his horse and headed down the hill towards the farm. Salvatore thought that the Lipiani situation was rather incredible. Being wealthy, Lipiani surely wouldn't need the money. After all, the men were good friends with Lipiani, especially Michael. Why would he do such a thing? Did he have a grudge against one of the men? Salvatore doubted it. Was it greed? Was Lipiani in some sort of trouble himself? Why?

Surely Lipiani must have realized that they would all be arrested, probably killed. Could a man that one liked, that one trusted and respected, want the death of many of his friends? Merely for some sum of money? There must be some factor, some situation that caused him to act this way, thought Salvatore.

Lipiani had acted, though, and betrayed his friends. Fro this, he must die. Friendship and trust is a person's most valuable asset, thought Salvatore. It is what separates men from wild animals. It is the all-important necessity of life, a quasi-religious relationship that must not be violated. In a very real sense, to Salvatore, friendship was more important than life itself.

As he continued to think about Lipiani, he noticed that the door of the house was open. Feeling that he was about to witness something horrible, Salvatore quickened his pace and began galloping for the house.

His pulse accelerated as he came closer to the house. At first, he thought he saw a large sack lying by the door. When he realized that it was a body, his heart began pounding loudly; fear swept through his body as a sudden wind kicked dust high in the free air.

It was Tramontane. Jumping off his horse, Salvatore walked over towards the dead farmer. His hands and feet were still tied together. The entire top portion of his head was missing and pools of blood accented his destroyed body.

"Some pig shot him in the head while he was tied up," muttered the paralyzed Salvatore. Sitting down on the ground, he began shaking uncontrollably. Not wanting to enter the house, he continued to gaze at the farmer for several minutes.

A horse neighed. Salvatore snapped out of his trance, still trembling. Slowly getting to his feet, he walked hesitantly toward the door. It was indeed ajar.

Breaking out in a cold sweat, Salvatore walked into the house. The parlor was in shambles. Glasses and plates were broken about the room. A small pool of wine had formed on the floor immediately below the table. Shattered wine flasks lay on the table. Several paintings were slashed as was nearly all the furniture.

Salvatore walked over to a chair and removed a half empty bottle of wine that was placed on the chair. Sitting down, he put the bottle on the ground, then picked it up again. Gulping down the wine, the terrified Salvatore saw the sun raise its ugly head over the small hill where the others were waiting.

He wanted to run out the door. Knowing where Maria would be, he still refused to go see her. The wine was beginning to soften the hard edges of the present as his body suddenly realized that it lacked sleep. Salvatore's mind, however, was far from drowsy.

Suddenly, he jumped up and ran out the door. Stopping as he saw Tramontane's body, he sat down on the ground and began weeping. A light wind was beginning to make the door sway.

The sunlight was unbearable. It burned his eyes; it

reminded him that he was alive by draining the alcoholic effects of the wine out of his body. Salvatore went back into the house and sat down on the chair again. Wiping the sweat off of his brow, he reached for the bottle and began gulping down its contents. Somehow he hoped that the wine would make him forget about Maria. It wouldn't.

Lipiani's image formed in Salvatore's brain. The hatred he felt for the man was pure, uncontrollable and unemotional. Salvatore felt that Maria would destroy him. He couldn't face her, he thought.

"My God!" he suddenly screamed.

It took Salvatore nearly one hour to generate enough will power to see Maria. As he rose from his chair, he rubbed his sweaty hands through his hair, then he turned towards the hallway determined to see her.

The walls confronted his drunken state as large obstacles. They were momentarily protecting him from what he was to see, but they were impeding his travel. As he approached her bedroom, Salvatore stopped. Breathing heavily, he forced himself to enter the room.

Maria lay on the bed dead. Her hands were tied above her head; her feet to the bedposts. Her jaw was smashed, her face and body - a bloody-stained battleground of destruction. There were finger marks on her throat; Maria stared open-mouth and wide-eyed at her ceiling. She would do that for eternity.

The sight was much more horrid than Salvatore could have ever imagined. Dropping to his knees, he began crying angrily as his entire body went into convulsions.

For minutes at a time, Salvatore's mind would blank out entirely. He welcomed such moments, but they became less frequent as the sun became stronger and higher.

He stood up and looked at her. The leaves of the large tree outside her window were causing the sunlight to dance furiously on her battered body. Salvatore walked over to her and cut the ropes off her wrists and ankles. She was stiff, very stiff.

Picking up a blanket from the ground, he wrapped her body as if trying to hide her many deep wounds. This would be too much for Michael, thought Salvatore as he gazed out the window at the burning sunlight. Although the light burned his eyes, he forced himself to stare at it as if he were being relieved by the pain.

Finally, after several minutes, he suddenly walked out of the room. Walking slowly to the chair, he sat down and resumed' consuming the wine. He hoped the images would fade.

By the time the others had arrived, Salvatore was quite drunk. As Carmine Bellaria's shocked face made contact with his, Salvatore exploded into a stream of bitter tears.

Running to Maria's room, Bellaria let out a loud scream which brought the other men into her room.

"Those pigs!" screamed Carmine Bellaria as he entered the parlor shaking like a madman. "My God, those pigs!" He began to cry.

The men sat around the house in silence for several hours. Aimlessly, they would look at various items in the house. Drinking heavily, they soon became drunk enough to momentarily forget their present.

"What are we going to do?" asked Carmine Bellaria as he looked nervously around, realizing that he had cracked the silence.

"I'm going home," said Salvatore coldly.

"Are you crazy? They'll kill you. Don't you realize what they have done here?"

"Yes, but I don't care. I'm going home to see my wife before I die. I have to see her, don't you see?"

"Everything is so horrible. What happened to life when it was so simple? How beautiful the work at the mines now seems. Now, we sit waiting for death to come to us. What are we to do?" asked Caro.

"Leave."

"Leave? Where, where are we to go?"

"America. Yes, America. It will be different there."

"What will make it different?" asked Carmine, doubtful of Salvatore's statement.

"Life is different there. We are too old, this island is too strong - we can't win this war. We must surrender."

"I love Sicily, though."

"Then leave. Do it now before she kills your spirit. Do it now!" exclaimed Salvatore excitedly.

"I suppose we should bury them," said Carmine after several minutes of silence.

Nodding, Salvatore let out a loud sigh, and then he stood up.

"I'm going home," he smiled, "Grazia, wait for me, I'll be there soon." He walked towards Maria's room.

The men prepared the Tramontane bodies for travel

to the cemetery. It seemed to Salvatore that he and the others were refusing to suffer any longer. The hot sun drained away all their emotions. Sicily had drained away their lives.

"What will you all do?" asked Salvatore as they had completed the task of preparing the farmer and his wife.

"We will wait for Michael, Cangeliera, and my brother," said Carmine Bellaria. "If you decide to rejoin us, we will be by Villarosa in a week, we'll come and get you, if you wish."

"If I'm alive," smiled Salvatore.

"Yes, if any of us are alive."

"Tell Michael to come see me right away. Don't tell him of what you saw here. Tell him that Maria is at my house."

"Yes, of course."

Salvatore shook everyone's hand and hoped that everyone would be careful. After several minutes of friendly salutations, Salvatore mounted his horse and headed for Villarosa.

It seemed like years since he had seen Grazia. With all the dying that was taking place around him, Salvatore felt a tremendous need to see his wife before anything happened to him. Not caring about the risks involved, Salvatore thought only of his family and proceeded onwards towards Villarosa.

The late afternoon sun was beginning to relax its burning tentacles as a cool, light breeze swept across the land. Salvatore welcomed the breeze as he welcomed the thoughts of a peaceful youth surrounded by great moments of happiness.

Michael and Franco and Salvatore the terrible trio, thought Salvatore, were now miles apart. Death had split the group as had misery and hunger. What was left in life wondered Salvatore as his horse clip clopped towards Villarosa.

Countless images of the past swirled about his numbing head. Baptista's characteristic walk that had accompanied those beautiful carefree days of Salvatore's youth seemed so distant now. Baptista was dead, as was Franco, the Tramontano's, Michael's family, Spilatieri, and probably by now Lipiani.

Death had not really acquainted itself with Salvatore's world until very recently. As a child and as a man, Salvatore had always seen others lament the sudden departure of a loved one, but he had never felt death's presence around him until Baptista had died, and then his father, Franco, and Spilatieri. Like a locomotive pulling out of a station, death's wheels were constantly accelerating.

Baptista had died not more than two years after Salvatore had bought her. It was one of those rainy March days that found Salvatore and Baptista slowly descending a hill. Slipping on the wet rocks, the horse reeled on her back legs and consequently threw Salvatore off her back. Continuing to run wildly down the steep incline, she fell off the edge of the hill down some three hundred feet to her death.

It was a severe blow to Salvatore. For weeks he wouldn't talk to anyone, nor would he look for work.

Michael and Franco, truly worried about his condition, attempted futilely to persuade Salvatore to come with them to the mines. Finally, when his father died two weeks later, he snapped out of his lethargic state. He joined them at the mines.

Salvatore thought he could see the outline of Villarosa. The town, perched on a small hill, greeted him with its familiar streets. He could barely wait to see his house, his wife and his children.

As he entered the village, he slowly proceeded towards his house. Looking at every possible sight, he acted as though this may be his final voyage through the village that had watched him grow from a happy boy to a miserable man. The various sights brought back memories, fond memories of his youth which seemed so remote, so unreal that Salvatore couldn't quite grasp whether the memories were in fact real.

Passing the small church where he had been baptized and married, an eerie sadness crept through his body. The early evening light seemed to suggest death in the semi-deserted village.

Salvatore quickened his pace. He wanted only to see Grazia. Forget the memories.

"Come on," he whispered to his horse, who broke into a gallop.

After several minutes, he raced to the bottom of the hill. Slowing down, he continued up the hill, cherishing every sight in his path. The small garden was still well kept. Smoke was rising from his chimney.

Dismounting, he raced into the house.

"Grazia," he yelled as he saw her sad eyes turn from the stove towards his. She was wearing black and her eyes, her eyes had an incredible, still look to them that frightened him.

Breaking out in a cold sweat, Salvatore's pulse quickened as he wondered whose death she was mourning. They hadn't stopped staring at each other. Salvatore's pleading eyes were begging for the nightmare to be over; Grazia's sad eyes were convincing him that it wouldn't end.

"What ... what is it?" he stammered.

She didn't answer. Grazia continued to stare at him, but her eyes began to fill up with tears as she began to tremble. The boiling water behind her on the stove was whistling loudly to be turned off, but to no avail.

"Help me," she gasped as he ran to her. She immediately burst out crying. Salvatore could feel her intense pain. Looking around the house for his children, he held Grazia close to him as she let out her bottled up emotions in a torrent of tears.

Having seen his children, Salvatore knew instantly who had died. The only other person who could have meant so much to Grazia was her brother, Michael.

"Michael?" he asked as his entire body convulsed.

"Michael?" he repeated hoping that she would deny it, knowing that she wouldn't.

"They killed him!" she suddenly screamed so loudly that Salvatore jumped in fright. Her voice resonated hatred, a passion she had never displayed.

"Who?" asked Salvatore as his insides were churning

with anger. "Who killed him?"

"Cangeliera and Santo Bellaria," whispered Lucio apologetically. "Bellaria killed himself this morning. The Gendarmes are looking for Cangeliera."

"What?" screamed Salvatore totally confused. "What are you saying?" he asked as he helped Grazia to a chair. Once seated, he went to Lucio, "What for?"

"They thought he had done some crime-"

"Go on, continue," interjected Salvatore as Lucio attempted to explain that he didn't know what crime Michael had been accused of.

"Well, anyway, they killed him and Bellaria went to Delvecchio to get the money. He was arrested and beaten because the lieutenant knew that Cangeliera was guilty and not Michael. Delvecchio and the lieutenant wanted to know where Cangeliera was-"

"Did he tell him?" asked Salvatore coldly.

"Yes, but I don't know what he said. Anyway they brought Bellaria here in town and he killed himself. They left an hour ago for Caltanissetta-"

"I know where he is," said Salvatore coldly. I'm going after him'."

"No!" screamed Grazia jumping from her chair. "You can't do that, you'll get killed! I can't stand anymore deaths, I'll die. Please," she pleaded, "don't go. They'll get him-"

"He was my best friend," said Salvatore calmly. "I must avenge his death."

"He was my brother!" she screamed. "Don't you think I feel the same way?"

"Grazia, Michael would have done it for me. I can't let him down. Don't you see, I have no pride left, no future, no friends. Everyone is dead. My spirit is dead. I must do it!" he exclaimed visibly excited. "I can't let him down like this."

Realizing that nothing could stop him, Grazia slowly walked back to the stove and turned it off. Salvatore looked at her in silence, and then looked at his children.

"I'm sorry, but I must do this. Someday you will understand," he said tearfully as he walked out the door. He didn't look back.

Night had spread its dark wings over Villarosa. Salvatore quickly mounted his horse, and galloped away, fearing that he wouldn't be able to face his family much longer. The village whisked by him as the tears, the hatred, and the anger he felt combined into supreme determination. Recklessly, he raced through the village, nearly running down several people.

Not caring if he was spotted, he abandoned caution entirely and raced for Cangeliera's hideout, desperately hoping he would reach it before Delvecchio and the Gendarmes did. He pushed all other things aside.

Riding into the dark, humid night, he thought over and over of how he was going to kill Cangeliera. That ruthless bastard, thought Salvatore, will wish he had never been born.

The first lights of the new dawn were seen by Salvatore as he approached the final hill before the small valley where Cangeliera was located. The Gendarmes were already there.

From Salvatore's vantage point, he could see two Gendarmes at the top of the hill, laying on their stomachs, spying on Cangeliera. The remainder of the Gendarmes was spreading out in a large circle.

Panic-stricken, Salvatore decided he could approach the house from the south side. The woods there would offer him some sort of protection. Dismounting some eight-hundred yards from the Gendarmes, Salvatore began walking in a giant arc to reach the woods. As he entered the woods, he found himself close to the Gendarmes. He decided to stop and see what they were doing.

"Corporal," barked Pavesi. "Make sure nobody shoots him. Is that understood? Corporal?" he continued as the corporal had turned around. "Make sure he is fully surrounded."

"Yes sir," said the corporal who ran off to execute Pavesi's orders.

"I want to kill that bastard!" exclaimed Pavesi to Delvecchio who was looking up the hill at one of the scouts who was fast approaching them.

"What's the matter?" asked Pavesi.

"Look, the scout is coming down the hill," answered Delvecchio.

"Lieutenant Pavesi," said the scout excitedly. "He is outside the house, sitting under a fig tree."

"Perfect," smiled Pavesi, "just perfect."

"Not too bad," said Delvecchio teasingly.

"Go back up there!" ordered Pavesi visibly excited. Motioning for the corporal to come to him, Pavesi planned his next move.

"Very slowly, I want all of the men to crawl up the hill, and then, when I yell to Cangeliera, I want all of the men to reveal themselves pointing their rifles at him. Understood?" asked Pavesi.

Salvatore realized that he didn't have much time left. Running through the woods, he quickly moved up the hill hoping to find an opening in the woods that would enable him to see Cangeliera. Searching desperately, he finally found a small niche in the woods that looked down on the valley. He could distinctly see Cangeliera who, seated under a tree, was passing the time aimlessly away.

Aiming his rifle at Cangeliera's midsection, Salvatore sighed and readied himself. Suddenly he felt his gun being pulled out of his hands as three Gendarmes wrestled with him.

In larger numbers, the Gendarmes were able to take the gun away from him and forced him to walk back towards Pavesi and Delvecchio's location.

"Well look who we have here!" smiled Delvecchio.

"He was about to shoot Cangeliera when we caught him," said a gendarme proudly.

"I see that Cangeliera has many enemies," said Pavesi sourly.

"The pleasure will be mine, though," he continued. "You may watch if you want."

"Just kill him, that's all I want," said Salvatore coldly. "Kill the bastard!"

"Why do you want him dead?" asked Delvecchio.

"He murdered my best friend."

Delvecchio thought it most prudent to drop the conversation, so he encouraged Pavesi to get on with the task at hand.

Quietly, Pavesi, Delvecchio, Salvatore and three other Gendarmes moved up the hill. Once at the top, Pavesi yelled:, "Stefano Cangeliera!"

Cangeliera jumped to his feet, startled by the voice. As he recognized Pavesi, he saw many Gendarmes; he was completely surrounded.

"What are you doing?" asked Cangeliera in the direction of Pavesi.

Pavesi laughed loudly for several long moments.

"I'm going to kill you, you son of a whore:" he exclaimed suddenly.

Cangeliera knew he was finished. There was no possible avenue of escape; death was imminent. He looked up at the bright early morning sun and smiled. His time had come, he might as well take it like a man, he thought.

"Hey Pavesi, will you grant me a few last words?" asked Cangeliera smiling happily.

"Sure," laughed Pavesi puzzled by Cangeliera's expression.

"I want you all to know," yelled Cangeliera, "that Marina has a nice sweet ass that I busted wide open with my-"

"SHOOT HIM!" screamed Pavesi out of control. "Shot him now!" he yelled as bullets ripped through Cangeliera's body.

Silence spread over the small valley. Cangeliera's blood smeared body lay demolished on the ground. The hot sun blasted its burning messages onto the morbid scene.

"You," said Delvecchio to Salvatore after several minutes. "What is your name?"

"Salvatore Campo," he answered coldly

"Did you hear -what happened this morning?" asked Delvecchio nonchalantly.

"No, I don't care either."

"It's over my friend. All the Gendarmes are coming back to Sicily. The war is over. I heard it this morning on the radio," said Delvecchio happily.

Nodding his head, Salvatore turned around and walked slowly down the hill.

Pavesi's truck convoy beat Salvatore and his quick horse to the place where the maimed Cangeliera had waited for Bellaria. Salvatore called it quits now, anxious only to rejoin his family. He walked openly from behind a cluster of arbor vitae which concealed him from view. He was unarmed and his sweaty steed followed closely behind. Pavesi's second-in-command stopped Salvatore, manacled him and shoved him brutally toward his chief.

Salvatore offered no resistance. Pavesi said to Salvatore, "You're a dead man, Salvatore Campo. What trick do you have up your sleeve now that you pay us this surprised visit?"

"No trick, Pavesi, I came as you did to kill this swine."

Pavesi struck Salvatore on the bridge of the nose with his gloved palm.

"Lieutenant Pavesi, you simple peasant bastard, I command soldiers here, you failure, not a band of stupid gangsters as you do. Salvatore Campo, you should have known when you started this game that I would be the victor. How dare you for a moment think you could pull this shit in my jurisdiction?"

Salvatore didn't answer and Pavesi grew infuriated.

"All the chief conspirators are dead, except you Signer Campo. You must die so I can wipe the slate clean in my report."

Pavesi hated Salvatore's steel-gray eyes. They saw right through him. They saw a frightened child who masqueraded behind the brass buttons and a chest full of badges and medals. Pavesi withdrew his Beretta pistol awkwardly from its yellow leather holster and aimed it at Salvatore's temple. Salvatore's expression remained unchanged as he told Pavesi to go ahead and shoot.

"You have finished my work for me, Pavesi. I came here for the same reason you did, to kill this miserable soul."

Pavesi continued the dialogue before the onlookers. No one honestly knew this encounter would conclude.

When Delvecchio saw Pavesi's gun pointed at close range to Salvatore's right temple, he rushed behind his lackey and smacked him behind the neck knocking off his cap.

"You dumb ass, this man is more of a man than you can ever wish to be. He could have killed you in ambush and us too if he wanted. You'll probably find his shotgun behind the bushes he came out of."

Pavesi picked up his hat and for a minute toyed with the idea of shooting Delvecchio.

"You would love to kill me, right, you God damn coward. I own you, you tin soldier and never forget that for a moment. I own your ass. Sergeant, take that man and lock him up. We'll let the law decide his fate, not chief executioner here."

Now Delvecchio wasn't going made with compassion. He realized that his life and fortune were inextricably tied up with the farmers and workers in the area. No purpose could be served by killing Salvatore.

Salvatore Campo was much thought of in these parts. Pavesi was hated. Delvecchio needed to save Campo from Pavesi to get back into the good graces of the people.

Campo was placed in the dungeon prison of the town's city hall to await the traveling judge's appearance in September. Campo was charged solely with the break-in of the granary. Pavesi made daily visits to the cell block to taunt Salvatore.

He instructed the jail keeper not to remove the excrement pot and feed him the rottenest of food or he would get him dismissed from his civil service post. The official complied when Pavesi was present, but disobeyed the orders when Pavesi left.

Once Pavesi tempted Salvatore with a story that the judge appointed to hear his case was a hanging judge. Pavesi admitted that Salvatore's presence in his jurisdiction undermined his authority since the men witnessed Delvecchio's treatment of him. Pavesi feared that Salvatore would recount this episode to disgrace him. Pavesi offered him a whore, money, and a gun to escape with. Salvatore was no fool. He knew that Pavesi had one of his men stationed behind the city hall courtyard ready to shoot Salvatore as a fugitive from justice once he showed himself in the open.

The entire populace crammed the make-shift court-room in the school-house the day of the trial. The chief prosecutor pushed for a life's sentence in compliance with the threatened demands Pavesi had made to him in private. The forceful prosecutor read the list of offenses in addition to the grand theft of wheat from the town's granary. The judge, a landed aristocrat himself listened intently to the litany of crimes Salvatore participated in.

Salvatore had no lawyer and threw himself at the mer-cy of the judge. Delvecchio sensed Pavesi's hand both in the prosecutor's indictment and in the choice of the men to decide the case. Delvecchio asked the jurist for the right to speak in defense of Salvatore Campo. What bet-ter time to be considered the champion of his people! Salvatore was no threat to him; it was just that Pavesi couldn't tolerate his physical presence in his district.

Delvecchio went straight to the point.

"Your honor, this man, Salvatore Campo, assisted us in tracking down and killing the worst member of the pack of brigands who terrorized this region during the war. The man we captured and killed was scum, not fit to live close to my friends and workers of this province. Even Lieutenant Pavesi will attest to the part Salvatore Campo played in the capture."

Pavesi's face reddened. The judge thought Delvecchio was finished, but Delvecchio continued.

"Campo is no animal, lie is an honorable man who only did what he did to care for his family. He had no way of knowing that some of his friends would go so sour."

Pavesi rose and fled the courtroom.

Salvatore Campo was sentenced to serve twenty years in a prison work camp in Sardinia. He was paroled after fifteen years.

Two men planned to catch the noon express this day from Messina to Palermo. Colonel Pavesi, recently appointed federal police officers in control of Lower Sicily, was on route to his varonial mansion on his father-in-law's estate. Salvatore Campo, recently released from a penal colony in Sardinia, returned to his Grazia and grown children.

Both men enjoyed the prime of their lives. Colonel Pavesi followed a physical exercise plan to combat bureaucratic roundness of his hips and buttocks and stay imperially trim to do justice to his regal attire. Pavesi's weakness for young women motivated him to stem any signs of natural aging. He used women as pawns in any criminal matter, in exchange for a sexual favor from a man's woman or daughter, Pavesi would lighten up or dismiss police action against him, depending on how the woman satisfied him.

Everyone in his district knew about Pavesi's eyes for local woman and, strangely, it caused conspirators to plan their illegalities more skillfully than ever not to encounter the lecherous Pavesi. Baron Delvecchio stopped trying to convert Pavesi's amorous ways, as Pavesi assisted

224

his father-in-law in maintaining his firm control and exploitation of the peasants. Pavesi's wife never recovered from her rape and assault and grew to detest the feel of a man's loins upon her. Her indulgent father spent a fortune to return his nervous daughter to normal, to the point where she could at least have a child. The daughter occupied herself with daily mass, fanatic cleaning of her own apartment, and keeping flawless, meticulous books for her father's business adventure.

Salvatore Campo's fifteen years as a gardener for the penal colony warden's private residence toughened his body. Not one ounce of fat adorned his athletic build. The combination of silvery hair and deeply tanned face gave him the appearance of a former Olympian. Living in the livery stable adjacent to the warden's home allowed Salvatore full access to the home itself. Salvatore was a trustee. The warden's wife, a former teacher, permitted Salvatore to join her tutorial sessions for her own children. Salvatore proved to be an apt student, with a natural ear for language and a flair for beautiful penmanship. He ate with the domestic help and the family doctor cared for the normal maladies which troubled his middle ages.

Salvatore missed his own family deeply, but his association with the warden's family kept him from being consumed with hate and revenge. The past was over and Salvatore thought only of salvaging the future and dedicating his remaining days to his own family.

Warden Perone placed no restrictions on his correspondence with Grazia and the flow of mail and occasionally photographs kept him aware of everything happening to his loved-ones.

The only time thoughts of killing Pavesi overcame him occurred when the warden's family was on a holiday and Pavesi was returned to the prison compound. The center aisle between the rows of cells was made of cobblestones. The turnkeys studded heels made a metallic click on the floor as he checked the cells at night. Salvatore would place his powerful hands over his ears to block out the sound which he imagined said kill, kill, kill. Plotting, revenge, and retribution were behind him. Only this metallic sound heard while in his cell rekindled the darker side every Sicilian has in his blood when he has been wronged and un-avenged.

Pavesi, on the other hand, had plans for Salvatore. Pavesi could never forget the humiliation he felt when his father-in-law cuffed him on the neck and berated him as a fumbling child when he wanted to kill Salvatore.

Salvatore showed no fear of Pavesi when he arrived at the farm too late to kill Cangeliera. Pavesi could stand no man he couldn't intimidate. Pavesi planned to crush Salvatore once and for all. He would warn the mine company, the pasta factory, and the new chemical plant that hiring Salvatore would mean a slight to their police superintendent. Pavesi had done all he could to red-tape what assistance the government might extend to the Campo family during Salvatore's incarceration.

Grazia never mentioned Pavesi's part in sabotaging her family in her letters. What good could that do? Friends and relatives offered what help they could do keep the Campo family intact.

Pavesi traveled first-class in the front car. He grew restless and decided to amble through the ten car train. He still loved to see the people's reactions when they gazed at his federal uniform. Some avoided eye contact conspicuously; others made shows of obsequiousness. Pavesi had once made an important arrest on the train of a parish priest wanted for smuggling gold to Germany and France without paying the necessary duties and taxes.

Nothing caught his attention as he strode through the cars. As he reached the last car, he decided to remain on the platform to enjoy a stogie and watch the landscape slip away. Even he couldn't stand the pungent aroma of the wine-soaked stogie he had been addicted to. He pulled a silver case from his breast pocket to extract a fresh stogie. He laid his shiny, black leather gloves on the thick wooden railing. The sun's rays reflected brilliantly off these handsome gloves.

Salvatore hadn't noticed the conspicuous figure of the police officer wending his way through his car. Salvatore had been preoccupied staring at a little child nursing from his mother's bounteous breasts. The scene filled Salvatore with great joy as he recaptured those times when he watched his own Grazia suckle her children. No one else occupied the last car.

Salvatore needed to stretch his legs. Arthritis from too many years in the damp sulfur mines had found its way into both knees. Salvatore relieved the ache by standing and flexing at the knees. He too entertained the same wish as Pavesi to catch some fresh air and gaze at the vegetated Sicilian countryside. Salvatore opened the half-glass steel door noiselessly out of respect for the dozing mother and child in the front portion of the speeding car.

Salvatore noticed the shiny black gloves resting on the railing. His gaze lifted slowly from the gloves to take in the full form of his arch enemy, Pavesi.

Maria and Baron Delvecchio's face, Spilatieri's face, and Cangeliera's face formed a collage. The metallic ring of the turnkey's boots on the cobblestone floor pounded on his ear; kill — kill — kill.

As Etna erupts with no warning to the village dwellers nestled on her mantle, as the wolf devours the snow-white lamb who has strayed too far from the flock, Salvatore's two-powerful arms pushed the form of Pavesi over the guardrail just as the train passed over the turgid river which emptied into the Sasso basin, the same river the swallowed Michael's wife and two precious children. Pavesi never realized what hit him from behind as his body hit the rails and bounded over the side of the bridge into the river. He was dead before his body touched the yellow, brown water.

Salvatore seized the fine leather gloves and threw them into the churning river also to signify the end of Pavesi' s reign of terror and brutality over a people better off without him. As the train slowed down to negotiate a dangerous bend in the track, Salvatore jumped from the rear platform. Salvatore estimated that he was twenty miles from his home town. Grazia had no idea that he left prison three days earlier than expected. He had much to see of the land that had changed much in the fifteen years he spent in jail. No need to be on the same train that Pavesi's family awaited at the ancient town train depot.

Salvatore trekked southward a complete man. He had his health, his family, his self-respect and honor, enough raw materials to start a-new in a distant land called America he had read so much about in the warden's personal library.

Thereafter, he went to the United States of America to join his family in Philadelphia, Pennsylvania. At seventy-five years old, Salvatore Campo lives comfortably with his wife, children and grandchildren. His two children, Calogero and Lucio are successful business men who still send money to Franco's widow in Sicily.

CPSIA information can be obtained at www.ICGtesting.com
Printed in the USA
BVOW072108290413

319416BV00001B/3/P